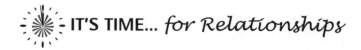
IT'S TIME... *for Relationships*

It's Time...
for Relationships
How spiritual wisdom can
bring freedom in relationships

Aruna Ladva

BRAHMA KUMARIS

BKIS

IT'S TIME ... FOR RELATIONSHIPS
How spiritual wisdom can bring freedom in relationships
Aruna Ladva

Copyright © 2013 BKIS Publications, London

PRINT ISBN 978-1-886872-39-4
KINDLE ISBN 978-1-886872-40-0
EPUB ISBN 978-1-886872-41-7

First published in 2013 by Brahma Kumaris Information Services Ltd,
Global Co-operation House, 65 Pound Lane, London, NW10 2HH
Website: www.inspiredstillness.com
E-mail: enquiries@bkpublications.com

The right of Aruna Ladva to be identified as the Author of the Work
has been asserted by her in accordance with the Copyright, Designs
and Patents Act 1988.

1 3 5 7 9 10 8 6 4 2

Illustrations by kind courtesy Mr Joachim Debarge
Designed by Makar Publishing Production, Edinburgh
Printed by CPI Group (UK) Ltd., Croydon, CR0 4YY

To the spiritual explorers around the world who, like myself, appreciate the inner journey which enables us to reach our inner wisdom and inner peace.

Contents

Contents

Introduction

It's no coincidence that you have picked up this book. This book is for those who are searching for truth and want to look deeper into their soul. So, if you are tired of quick fixes, and wish to get to the root of your relationship problems, then this book is for you.

I also consider myself to be on a spiritual journey. I teach meditation and I continually work on the 'self', aiming to make improvements on a daily basis. I work to develop inner calm, clear thinking and personal well-being and I teach and encourage others to do the same. For the past 36 years I have been on a spiritual journey with the Brahma Kumaris World Spiritual University. They are an international meditation group with over 8,500 branches in more than 110 countries. I have been privileged to help establish a few of those branches.

The Brahma Kumaris acknowledge the intrinsic goodness within everyone and they offer people a place to go for lifelong learning, regardless of their religion or spiritual background. The organisation helps people to explore their own spirituality through the practice of Raja Yoga meditation.

Raja Yoga is a form of silent meditation that helps bring the mind and emotions into balance, which in turn helps you to develop knowledge and wisdom and gain a deep understanding of the self. Practising Raja Yoga meditation gives you the power to exercise choice over thoughts, feelings and responses. In time this practice becomes a natural part of your awareness, transforming how you see yourself and your relationships. It offers a practical understanding of spirituality, and you can take as much or as little as you wish to help you on your own journey.

Although I have been practising Raja Yoga meditation for many years, I began writing so that I could understand things better for myself. Later, I began sharing my writing with a small group of meditators who appreciated receiving some weekly thoughts. I then started a blog, so that I could share my thoughts with a wider audience. I called my blog 'It's Time' because I felt it was time for us to wake up, open our eyes and 'get real' about life.

My inspiration for the blog articles has often arisen out of situations and circumstances I have encountered on my journey, and often as a result of some form of sacrifice, expense or pain. Thus, the articles are written from the heart and from my honest experience.

I hardly paid attention to promoting the articles or my blog, but they seemed to take on an organic growth and followed their own journey to different corners of the globe. I was astounded when the statistics showed 17,000 hits to the blog within the first year. "That's more than a size of a concert hall", I thought to myself. Now, I've decided to share some of my articles from 'It's Time' in this book.

If you go to the blog you will find many articles on a variety of topics – much like a smorgasbord where you can pick and choose what you fancy. For this book I have chosen a selection of articles on relationships as this is a topic relevant to everyone. I have picked articles that look at what happens when relationships go wrong, how they need to be sustained and how we can bring closure when they finally end.

This book is by no means a definitive guide; it is more a compilation of some of my own reflections, observations and experiences collected on my own personal journey. Perhaps some of these thoughts will resonate with you.

You can read this book from start to finish, or open pages randomly to simply see what emerges for you. Whatever you

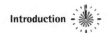

come across, I am sure it will be relevant for you at this point on your own journey.

At the end of each article there is a short paragraph entitled 'It's Time …'. This will help you to zoom into the essence of the article and walk away with some thoughts to reflect upon and digest. Many readers have shared their experience of how timely these messages were in their life. I hope they will help you too.

What are relationships?

The art of relating to others is perhaps the most important of all arts – it is the essence of how to live our life on this planet. We spend all of our life in relationships, but how many of those relationships are satisfying and good? Knowing just how much to give and take on all levels, to manage the differences in our personalities and to learn to forgive and move on are important skills that we need to understand and to harness. Whether at home, work or outdoors, we are always interacting with people. But what is the quality of our interactions with others? Do we invest the time and energy needed to create good relationships? Can we be open and compassionate or are we constantly defensive and selfish? The quality of our relationships is determined by the time, effort and trust we invest in them.

So, what is the most important relationship I will ever have? It is the relationship with myself. I need to give myself the space and time to get to know and understand myself; the quality of the relationship I have with my 'self' will reflect in the quality of my relationships with others. I was lucky that meditation became a part of my life from an early age and it continues to teach me to take responsibility for my own thoughts, feelings and actions. I realize that there is no one else to blame for where I am and how I feel. An important part of my practice is to constantly look in the mirror to see where I am going wrong and then to take action.

As I practised this approach to life and relationships I realized I was blaming others less and was able to manage my reactions and emotions more effectively. This brought with it a sense of self-confidence and an inner knowing even from a young age. I was grateful to meditation for connecting me with myself and also with God, who has been by my side as my best friend and companion since I was a child.

Raja Yoga meditation tells us we have all the resources we need within us to live more fulfilling lives. Love and generosity are part of the intrinsic nature of the soul. When we act from this place of fullness then we are able to relate to others and ourselves from a place of abundance, not emptiness.

When I remember and reconnect with my intrinsic goodness then I realize I am already whole. This profound feeling changes my perspective and outlook on life and I have the power to deal with situations more wisely.

Relationships can feel wonderful when they are smooth sailing, but when things go wrong it can change our whole mood and affect our behaviour and the way we feel about ourselves and others. When we respond in a more positive way to problems that is when we realise how far we have come on our journey.

The articles in this book take a closer look at relationships and how we relate to others. Are we supportive and kind or do we take from them selfishly? How can we be happier and more considerate in our relationships? What happens when things don't go the way we want and we encounter problems?

The articles offer a way of looking at situations from a different perspective, which may not be immediately apparent to us when we are in the situation at the time. By reflecting on those situations and how we responded to them we may prevent ourselves from falling into the old patterns of behaviour. Instead, with increased awareness and sensitivity we can make changes within ourselves to create different and more positive and meaningful outcomes next time.

This book is divided into two parts. The first part looks at our relationship with the 'self' and how we can develop and

nurture ourselves. The second part looks at our relationships with other people, including the things that annoy us,
how to resolve conflict and how to bring pure love into those
relationships.

IT'S TIME... to remember that we are all mirrors for each other;
we only see in others what we have in ourselves. So let us see
only the positive.

Part One...
Our relationship with ourselves

'I'

This single letter word has been the downfall of many an empire. Although the letter looks insignificant and isolated, and we may even feel sorry for it, this small word can carry such a huge weight of ego that it can swipe and kill anything in its path. Conquering the false 'I' of ego, is one of the first things we must do when we are on a spiritual journey. So, it's important to be aware of the consequences of using the word 'I' so that we are not deceived along the way.

The world of trade and commerce revolves around defending and buttressing the existence of the physical 'I'. Fashion and design, stock markets, the food industry and world of technology; each calls out to the ego by creating an atmosphere of competition, desire and fear. Countless billions of dollars are the prize but needless to say, this gives little attention to the development of the inner 'I'.

When we use the word 'I' do we stop to consider which 'I' we mean? 'I' is used to define the self, but which self are we referring to? Is it the one we see in the mirror, the 'I' of the physical form, or the one we feel we are on the inside – the soul – the real essence of who we are?

On a spiritual journey, our aim is to dissolve the body conscious ego and turn it into pure, untainted self-respect. But that will only happen when we get to know ourselves as a soul – a being of light and virtue. It is an illusion to think that we are just flesh and bone that will one day turn to dust or ashes. When we identify ourselves with the physical 'I', then this becomes our biggest mistake.

Raja Yoga shows simply how to return to the pure 'I' – the pure consciousness, the pure essence of being. This is the state in which we rediscover ourselves; unique and beautiful irrespective of the colour of the costume or mask we may wear. But, although we understand that before we can even consider enlightenment we have to have our physical needs such as food and shelter met, we continue to confuse the need of the body with greed.

The false 'I' exists in the mistaken belief that we are what we have; a body, possessions and our roles in life. We have forgotten that the life-force within the body makes everything tick. It's like adoring your fancy new cellphone but forgetting that it's useless if it's not charged.

Saying 'I' from the heart and feeling the deep qualities of the self within is quite different from focusing on our public status.

The world would be a different place if we related to each other through our inner qualities, and not through our status or profession and the ego of 'I'.

To make matters worse, we alternate 'I' with 'we'. This is a clever way of concealing the ego. We say that 'we' will do it, when it's really 'I' that wants to do it and claim all the credit. It's the false 'I' of pretence, the feeble and false humility. Because the conscience knows it's on an ego trip, the false 'I' involves an accomplice in its desires, in order to appease itself. When the collective 'we' is involved, the guilt caused by the ego is minimised.

The true 'I' is the master of our senses. But, instead of being the master of our senses and telling them what to do, we have become their slave. They are our masters, telling us what to eat, see, touch, taste and smell, sometimes even against our better judgement.

With every thought that is created due to the pull of the senses, we become body conscious. But, with every thought created based on our innate virtues of peace, love and truth, we reinforce soul consciousness. With the world pulling our senses more and more we have become accustomed to thinking we are simply a body. The mind will believe whatever it is told. As we lose sight of the truth of the soul, we also lose the unlimited power that goes with it, and so we start to believe that our power is limited to our physical body, or the strength that results from position and status.

Imagine a world where the 'I' of the ego is replaced by the real 'I' of true self-respect. The real 'I' would not feel the need to compete or seek to defend itself against perceived threats from others, whether from a hurtful glance or an aggressive nation. It would not demonstrate its lack of self-control by trying to control others. The real 'I' would not feel the need to turn inner pain into aggression and violence toward others. It would not be at the mercy of its own emotions or the negative energies around it, but would indeed be the master of its own destiny. The law of this world would be love, not fear.

IT'S TIME... to sit quietly, play some soft music and remind yourself that you are a pure and peaceful being, a being of light and truth. You are master of your body. Get in touch with your divine core, the purest and untouched part of yourself. From this seat of self-respect you can then tell your senses who is boss.

The inner voice

Our conscience, the inner voice of reason, acts as our inner compass providing us with our own personal navigation system. It can be our greatest friend if we only stop to listen and we ignore it at our peril. Much of the time we bury it, muffle it, or give it less importance in our life.

Our inner voice is our voice of wisdom. It speaks to us, providing clues and road maps to living life as it is meant to be lived: in accordance with the natural spiritual laws. It's a tool that steers us toward living in harmony with everything around us. It urges us to balance our lives by helping us measure what we say and do, and what not to say and do. It guides us to choose good over evil and to perform acts that give happiness over sorrow.

The primary objective of the conscience is to keep us safe within a space of peace and happiness. It prevents us from performing actions that will have a detrimental effect on others and ourselves. When we trust and follow our inner voice it ultimately awakens the mind to a purer awareness and a higher and more elevated consciousness.

The path of spirituality advocates that we nurture and listen to our conscience on a consistent basis. Mastery over the mind comes from listening, discriminating between right and wrong, and following through with the good. Religions advocate that we should 'follow' them, which only makes us followers and not leaders. It's wise to not get stuck in the dogma, but to look at the deeper spiritual values religions offer. The wisdom is buried deep within us, knocking quietly to get our

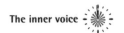

attention; we just need to spend some time listening to it.

If we return to the core values of our soul we will find that at the deepest level the conscience is pure and untouched, ultimately seeking only peace, love and happiness and wanting the same for others. This is why we have a natural ability to be able to separate good from evil, to want peace over war and know the difference between happiness and sorrow. Intrinsic to each of us is a memory chip that is never totally overwritten, no matter how bad or evil someone may appear to be on the surface.

Einstein often referred to the inner voice as the source of both moral and physical knowledge. Sometimes we do or say things that we know are not right and our conscience bites, reminding us that we have just gone against our own grain and violated our own deepest truth.

The restlessness we feel inside is the misalignment of our feelings, words and deeds. It is all sparked off with a feeling, and our feelings never lie. Uncomfortable feelings are the alarm bells of our conscience, which alert us to a possible

intruder who will upset our true state of being. There follows a moment of choice, and the soul then needs to find the power to follow through with the right action. But when it can't, we discover that we have given birth to a guilty conscience.

In his book *The Unconscious Civilization*, John Ralston Saul states that:

> "In contemporary developed nations many people have acquiesced in turning over their sense of right and wrong, their critical conscience, to technical experts ..."

This is certainly true in many instances where, as a consumer, we impulsively purchase without taking into account the limited resources of our planet. Have we lost our conscience? Are we simply living in the moment, without any moral obligation toward our descendants?

Sometimes we can make erroneous judgments. However, whether out of ignorance or out of wrong intentions, every individual is culpable for the misdeeds he commits. The law of action and reaction, sometimes called the law of karma, means that we are all responsible for the results of our own actions. We should therefore pay great attention to our thoughts and actions, for at some point we will have to repay our debts or repent for our misdeeds. Listen to your inner voice carefully.

Corporate Social Responsibility is a positive move in the area of cultivation of social or collective conscience. Increasingly, companies and entrepreneurs, and people like theme restaurateur Steven Schussler, who created the Rainforest Café, are exercising philanthropy as well as profitability. He states:

> "Helping others while helping yourself is not counter-productive – it can even be synergistic."

As we listen to our conscience we also uplift ourselves.

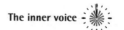

IT'S TIME... to listen to our inner voice and to not switch off the alarm when it rings. Our conscience is our friend, not our enemy. We need not fear it as it's there to help us live and die as a better person. World peace can only come when we understand and implement our moral obligation to the greater whole and that means that each one of us, as a fundamental part of the collective, needs to listen to our own conscience and to 'clean up our act' accordingly.

Ageless and timeless

'You are what you think' is an old adage, but do we ever stop to ponder its meaning? How, exactly, does this affect our attitude towards ageing?

We probably all know someone who is young at heart, in spite of the fact that their body tells a different story. Likewise, some people seem old before their time, or wise beyond their years. But, how old we are and how old we look, feel or behave is not the same thing.

Even science is now telling us that we age according to how we think! We are the only creatures that are aware of getting old and each of our thoughts, either conscious or unconscious, acts as a command that programmes every cell of the body. Our cells eavesdrop on our thoughts and respond accordingly. For example, the thoughts: 'I can't do what I used to' or 'I'm too old for that' will definitely come true for us. This is the reason why the face becomes a mirror of the mind: if you feel blissful, you have a happy persona.

To really understand this phenomenon, we need to step beyond the world of matter and into the metaphysical. While some may search for the fountain of eternal youth, those who are willing to learn from life know that we discover the real secrets of time when we begin to know our real selves; that unchanging eternal part of us, the soul.

In this timeless realm our notion of ageing changes. Young ones become mature, and the elderly become youthful as we step outside the bounds of time and free the self from all limitations.

The soul can never age; it is eternally young and also eternally wise. We should enjoy being the playful child, the caring parent, the masterful leader and the enlightened sage, as they are each a part of us.

We usually think of ourselves as merely physical beings, but this will create dismay or even fear at the appearance of yet another wrinkle, another ailment, or another passing year. Losing friends and loved ones increases the sense of our own impending mortality. When we forget our truth and purpose the journey of life can seem as if we are merely filling in time. The journey may be filled with a collection of experiences, both good and bad, but without truth and purpose it may seem that we are moving towards (literally) a dead end.

Contrast that with the thoughts of the spiritual traveller, who may describe himself as being ageless, but because he knows himself as a soul and that he is imperishable. The end of his body is not the end of his journey.

We are all spiritual travellers, whether we believe it or not. The meaning of life is not to 'do', but to 'be'. To experience and enjoy the moment we are in, as now it is truly the only moment that we ever have. Being in the 'now' actually connects us with our eternal self. In this place of certainty, change is no longer a threat: it is merely an expression of the continual flow. All is well, and all will be well. Fear is no longer inevitable, as every day becomes a celebration of life, every moment an event to be savoured and enjoyed as part of our learning and growing.

In soul consciousness the spiritual traveller, whose habit is to step beyond time and space, is free. The body becomes revived, recharged and revitalised simply through the choice of these empowering, nourishing and live-affirming thoughts.

At the end of the day, we know that we will only be around in our physical reality for as long as our destiny will allow. But, we can choose to make the most of every second and each moment becomes a preparation for the next step in the journey.

IT'S TIME... to move away from limited thinking and step into the unlimited where you are not bound by time and fear. Express yourself from your timeless qualities and respond to others in the same way. Most of all, know that you can't live in the past or the future, you can only live in the eternal 'now', so make the most of every second.

Take off your shoes

The removal of shoes before entering homes and holy places is common for many who live in warmer climates. But is it just for hygiene reasons? What does this really symbolize? Why has this tradition been handed down from generation to generation?

Shoes, most often made of leather, are a metaphor for the physical aspect of the human being; the leather of 'body consciousness'. As we enter a mosque, a church, a synagogue or a temple, no matter how rich or poor, we cannot carry our ego or arrogance with us, even if it's concealed in the cloak of our noble character. We have to leave all that at the door.

Body consciousness can come in many forms. For example, being over-concerned about the way we look (no wonder the beauty industry is a multi-billion dollar business), or needing to acquire and show off wealth and assets to keep up with the Joneses and inflate our position in the eyes of others. Body consciousness reveals itself to us in some of the following ways: complaining, criticising, commenting, cursing, and condemning. Judgement, jealousy and discontentment are very often the root of body consciousness.

The antithesis of this body conscious attitude is 'soul consciousness'. Or, rather, the antidote to this self-destructive behaviour is the state of soul consciousness where 'I', the real self, is completely calm, cool, content and comfortable inside. A feeling of satisfaction and security comes when we understand that all of our authentic, invisible assets are within us. For it is from this place that qualities of peace, love, joy, power, truth, creativity and compassion emerge.

In the eyes of God, we are all equal and transparent; there is only a disparity in rank when we look at the body. All religions suggest that the body is merely a veil of mud or dust covering the soul, also known as the spirit, ruh, or atma. Interestingly, the name atma, or atom, comes from the Greek 'atomos', which means indivisible: something that cannot be divided any further. Thus, when we are stripped to our essence, we are free of any fancy labels, brands or hallmarks of our heritage or education.

Similarly, as we arrive home, the act of taking off our shoes represents an un-layering: the transition from the variety of characters we play in our workplace to becoming ourselves once again.

Ironically, as we cast off the layers of ego that we have been comfortably hiding behind for so long, we become whole again. We are grounded, becoming one with our universal family. We accept ourselves and can accept others for who they are. We can begin to appreciate their real qualities as we begin to see the light of the soul of each and every one behind their physical costume.

This light cannot be weighed against gold or diamonds; it is measured in attributes. It's the virtues, or lack of them, that makes the soul either shine or become dull. With every layer of body consciousness that we uncover, we reveal another tier of virtue in the soul.

IT'S TIME... to take off your shoes. Get real. Be honest. Feel the ground you stand upon with no need for masks or masquerades. In meditation, practice being conscious of the light of the soul and you will automatically discard the mantle of body consciousness. It's similar to walking into a dark room; you do not attempt to chase away the darkness but simply switch on the light.

Valuing yourself

Everything you attract into your life is a reflection of what you feel you deserve, what you feel you are worth and how highly you value yourself in all areas of your life. The internalization of self-esteem is a process begun early in life and continues throughout. Because it is a process and not a destination, you can raise your self-esteem by understanding yourself and by increasing your self-worth.

Self-worth is the conviction that you are worthy of happiness. Self-worth is the way you talk to yourself about yourself, how you feel about yourself and the extent to which you think and feel you can cope with the situation in front of you. If you treat yourself well, other people will too. If you give across needy messages, people may not respect you and could also take advantage.

Self-worth gives birth to self-confidence. Self-confidence is an attitude and when used positively it allows the individual to have a positive yet realistic view of themselves and their situations. But it doesn't mean they will be able to do everything. Self-confident people trust their own abilities and have a general sense of control in their lives. Even when some of their expectations are not met, they continue to be positive and accept themselves. They nurture themselves. They manage their thoughts and don't allow weak or negative thoughts and feelings to creep in and sap their confidence.

People with little self-worth depend excessively on the approval of others in order to feel good about themselves. They tend to avoid taking risks because they fear failure. They generally do not expect to be successful. They often put themselves down and tend to discount or ignore compliments paid to them. By contrast, self-confident people are willing to risk the disapproval of others because they generally trust their own abilities. They don't feel they have to conform in order to be accepted.

Do you feel enthusiastic about yourself? Do you look in the mirror and say: "Yes, I like the person who looks back at me"? Are you thankful for your talents? Are you genuinely happy to be you or would you rather be living someone else's life? You have to live with yourself forever, so if you don't like yourself, who will?

Self-worth, or lack of it, permeates our work and our personal lives – it leaves a mark on everything we do. Cultivating self-worth means you deserve the best at every moment. However, overeating, drinking excessively, smoking and generally not being in control of yourself, or allowing others to be disrespectful toward you, are all signs of disrespecting oneself. In other words, your actions strongly affect your self-worth.

Ask yourself: what stops me from liking myself? What are the ways I hold myself back because of a lack of self-belief? What are the things I do in order to be liked by others? What are the things I tolerate or put up with because of a lack of self-worth? What are the things I will not forgive myself for? In what ways do I punish myself? For example, do I tolerate lateness, just to be liked? Do I punish myself by working longer hours or doing the jobs no one else likes to do? Do I overeat to bury my emotional pain?

Feelings of self-worth are quite distinct from ego. It is the knowledge and awareness of our own intrinsic uniqueness, beauty and value of the soul, not just the skills and abilities we have or our possessions, or the reputation we hold in the eyes of others. It is recognising that we deserve the best from life just because we exist and not because of what we do.

Here are some tips for increasing self-worth:

Self Evaluate
Learning to evaluate yourself independently will save you from depending on the opinions of others. Focus internally on how you feel about yourself. Manage your thoughts and stop giving away your personal power to others by seeking approval or recognition.

Emphasize Strengths
Give yourself credit for everything you try and do. In every saint there is a sinner and in every sinner there is a saint. Focus on feeding the saint.

Use Positive Self-Talk
There is constant chatter in your mind so make this positive. Talk to yourself with love and appreciation, not criticism and judgement. Remove toxic thoughts. When you catch yourself expecting perfection, remind yourself that you are doing your best.

Take Risks
See life as an adventure. Approach new experiences as opportunities to learn from rather than occasions to win or lose. Doing so opens you up to new possibilities and can increase your sense of self-acceptance. Not doing so turns every possibility into an opportunity for failure and inhibits personal growth.

Surround Yourself with Positive Images and Influences
Choose the people you wish to hang out with. Negative and demanding people drain your energy and don't help to increase your self-worth. Positive people with a healthy mindset are more inspirational.

Wipe the Slate Clean
A clear conscience is essential for self-worth. If we feel bad about things we have done in the past, we will, in subtle ways,

try to punish ourselves. Accidents often happen because we feel we deserve them. We can't change the past, but we can understand it and let go. Feeling bad about ourselves keeps us doing more bad things.

Tidy Up

Tidy up your house and your life. Clear out clutter from your space; things you have not used in the last year. If you value yourself and your time you will value your personal space and possessions and so will others. A tidy mind has few but focused thoughts, they are determined and powerful, and this is reflected within a tidy personal surrounding. A cluttered mind can only create clutter; a clear mind brings clarity.

IT'S TIME... to choose to treat yourself with complete respect. Forgive yourself for the mistakes you have made. The more you honour and respect yourself, the more others will too. To invite great people into your life, make yourself a great person to be with. You are worth it and you deserve it.

Coaching the mind

We live in a world where we have so many coaches, gurus, spiritual consultants and self-help books to help manage our minds, yet it seems practically impossible to focus on a single point for more than a few seconds. The mind is like mercury: slippery and hard to contain. Since our thoughts are the seeds of our actions, it is imperative that we get a hold over our own mind and begin coaching it before someone else does.

Taking responsibility for oneself is the key. Stop the blame game and take ownership of your thoughts; you are creating your thoughts, no one else. When you create waste thoughts, remember that no one is doing anything to you; you are the one giving your power away or allowing it to be taken from you. You are responsible for every thought you create, not your government, your schoolteachers or your mum and dad.

Stop the projection. The duty of the projector is to enlarge everything; it shows it in 3D with great glamour. In the same way, we begin with a single tiny thought and before we know it we blow it out of proportion and react by throwing it onto someone else. Nothing is really as big as it seems. Ask yourself: "Will this disagreement, dispute, or disruption really matter in a month, a year, or five years from now? Will it carry the same weight? Will I care as much then as I do now?"

Just as sports coaches use powerful, positive imagery and language to help the players visualise their goals and victory, in the same way, if we want to create a winning strategy in life, we have to create a positive vision of ourselves. We need to generate positive, powerful pictures of a healthy mind, body and spirit. If a coach constantly picks on the weaknesses of the players or the team he will likely lose his job very quickly. A coach's job is to identify the strengths and the weaknesses, and then focus on the strengths. When was the last time you patted yourself on the back for a job well done, or for being more tolerant, more charitable, more efficient?

The job of a life coach is to help their clients articulate their dreams, desires and aspirations, and to help them clarify their mission and purpose. Coaching our own mind means that we need to assess how well it is working, and focus on enhancing that which is positive. Ask yourself: "Do I talk to myself with compassion? Do I beat myself up for every mistake I make? Is my purpose clear to me? Am I making headway every day toward being the person I want to be?"

In some sports a lot of importance is given to correct breathing. The quality of our breathing is extremely important to our health and our quality of life. Equally, it is essential to ensure that the mind can breathe properly because the thoughts we create are oxygen for the mind. They can either be powerful or they can be weak and our attitudes and actions will follow suit. Thus, if our thoughts are not positive and pure, then we will not generate enough energy to make the changes we want to see in our life.

Finally, a coach ensures that his players don't procrastinate: they just do it, and do it now. If every exercise or affirmation were left to the next day we would not have exceptional athletes or achievers. Likewise, to stay creative and motivated, we need to coach our minds into taking action now, this minute. If we leave it until tomorrow it may never happen. Procrastination kills; it kills the idea, the motivation and the will, and we lose the power of the moment.

IT'S TIME... to recognise that you are the one who is running your mind and to lovingly, but firmly, coach it toward becoming fitter, more flexible, more positive and more powerful. This is the only way to really win in the game of life.

Soul worker

A soul worker is constantly striving for improvement and personal development. If one approaches life as an artist, considering all our experiences in life to be the tools with which to weave a perfect masterpiece, then life can be fun and creative, instead of a chore and a struggle.

An artist combines a variety of elements to produce the most perfect outcome. Take for example the florist who arranges an assortment of flowers to create an exquisite bouquet. The chef combines ingredients to create the most sumptuous feast. The tailor takes fabrics of various colours and textures, cuts them up and sews them into a stylish piece of clothing.

Just as plastic surgeons take the scalpel to flesh and remodel it to create a more desirable appearance, why can't we become the makers of our destiny and create the life we desire or aspire to? The greatest work of art has to be our ability to patch up the pieces of our broken heart and to make it whole again. Someone may have cracked that heart, others may have walked away with pieces of it and we may have lost some of those pieces along the way to people and places. But, we have to forgive, forget, let go and continue bridging, building and forging relationships despite any hurts felt along the way.

Soul work is an art; it's a way to become whole again. It's only when we look inside using our 'intro-vision' that we are able to re-evaluate the workings of our soul. We are then able to find other ways to view situations and to respond to them in different ways, rather than following the patterns we have built up and which are more readily available to us.

Working on any piece of art takes patience and perseverance. And we may revisit it several times before we are happy. The end result might be obvious in our mind and vision, but compared with the current reality, it may seem a long way away. For that we need patience.

Just like tailoring, sculpting, designing and cooking, perfecting the soul is an art that can take up an entire lifetime. As negative events around the world increase, there is increased demand on our patience, tolerance, kindness and compassion; our speed of adaptation and personal growth has to correspond with the changing times. Those with an archaic and fixed mindset may get left behind.

Artists are always confronted with critics. Some are genuinely constructive, while others criticize out of spite and jealousy. Whatever the nature of the criticism, a soul worker always approaches it positively, taking what is relevant and discarding what is not. Switch off the voice of self-doubt and amplify the voice of self-respect. Stay focused and in alignment with your vision.

Most artists suffer from blocks of one kind or another that may hinder their creativity. The greatest block for the soul is when it falls asleep or, worse, forgets how beautiful and magnificent it once was. We cannot strive for that which we have not yet known or experienced. So, if the soul worker's vision is a life of peace, happiness and abundance, then it's because the soul has experienced that and been there before.

When something is beautiful everyone takes a second look. Most people can easily discern between the good and the bad, the best and the worst; they want the finest and are ready to pay the price for it. The soul worker too has a sharp eye that can distinguish between the beauty and the beast within. We then just need the strength to conquer the beast and allow our beauty to shine.

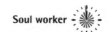

IT'S TIME... to take on your role of soul worker seriously and to look at the beauty within and let yourself shine. Paint your life and begin to get creative; bring out the colours, the shine and the imagination. Try to look at things from a different perspective and enjoy the drama of life around you. Let every scene and incident be the chisel and hammer that defines and refines the beauty of the idol within; you are that beauty, you are that soul.

Soul wear

Traditional attire bears such individuality that it not only tells us something about the wearer but it also reveals a lot about where they live, their environment and their social status. From time immemorial the quality, style and richness of clothes have reflected the social strata of a culture, whether distinguished by colours, fabrics or feathers.

By contrast, organizations and institutions such as schools, the military, a public service, or even a fast food outlet, all signal to us their roles and position in society by the uniforms they wear.

Today, many of us have fully embraced Western brand names; the designer label has now become a statement of 'where we are at'. In an attempt to assert our individuality we have unwittingly created a new uniform based on our purchasing power. Around us there is increasing evidence that our attire is often no longer based on cultural, or even moral values. Traditions are being eroded away and the sparkle and the glamour once reserved for kings and queens is evident in abundance in any shopping mall. There is nothing intrinsically wrong with owning or wearing a designer outfit, the question we need to ask ourselves is "Am I simply wearing the suit, or is the suit who I think I am?"

In this world of first impressions, the desire to make our mark is often irresistible. Our society's values condition and encourage us to judge by appearances and sometimes we look no further. However, if we only judge the book by its cover then imagine what we are missing. If we fail to see beyond the outer, embellished layer, then we cannot avail ourselves of the treasures that are contained within.

A spiritual journey is one where the seeker, with a desire to know the deepest truths, begins to peel away the layers to uncover their real essence. The special pilgrimage to Mecca advocates that men must give up their noble dress and wear a garment consisting of two sheets of white un-hemmed cloth. That is, to be simple in front of God: no ornaments, no pretence, no ego. The same is true for a pilgrim of any religion. As we remove our outer layers – the outer 'self' that we present to the world – we realize that deeper layers exist. The body is a dress, a costume that envelops the soul and the essence of who we are, and we need to discover our greatest treasures, which lie within it. Any pilgrimage also requires purity of mind. We can only focus on God when our attention is not pulled toward the costumes of others.

The wisdom embedded in the call to clothe the body in simple attire beckons us to elevate ourselves and go beyond matter to awaken our spiritual light. It reminds us that before God we are all essentially equal and that what will distinguish us from one another in the final reckoning is not artificial beauty, fame or glory but how pure our heart is. It is what we did for others, not how much we did in selfishness for ourselves. It is in how much we lived a life of real value.

IT'S TIME... to re-assess how you define yourself and how much you live by your deepest values of love and truth. As you begin to recognize your own real essence and to see the true depth and worth of the people around you, you will begin to create your own haute couture of high thinking and simple living.

Freedom of spirit

Have you ever wondered what it is that truly makes your spirit free? Some believe it is that dream job with better pay and prospects that is the highway to freedom. Others feel liberated in finding their 'other half'. Some want the government to step in and free them from their mortgage and tax payments. Real freedom is not about running off into the country or buying a plot on the moon. It's about freeing yourself from your internal demons or negativity.

Everyone wants to be free. Whether we are young or old, none of us likes the feeling of being trapped or confined – either physically or emotionally. Freedom speaks up, raises its head and voice and won't stop until it is heard.

But in the name of freedom we have actually set ourselves up in bondage. How? By giving away our power. If we want the government to fix our world, we give them the reins to govern our life. We relinquish our power to our spouse when we expect him or her to be the sole source of our fulfilment and happiness in life. We abdicate responsibility for our own life and, as a consequence, our own freedom is lost.

In the name of love we lose our individuality and thus our freedom of spirit. It's a catch-22 situation. We thirst for the love, trust and security of our partner, but we are not willing to put up with any investigative questioning of our whereabouts. Therefore, love also feels like a trap.

In personal relationships we surrender to the other in the name of trust. However, with each layer of submission we also relinquish personal power. While we are submitting we are also

being trapped. It is akin to being protected and restricted at the same time.

In sexual relationships there can be no give without take. The moment we have taken from our partner on any level – physical, emotional, or sexual – we are in debt to that soul to return the experience. There is no free lunch.

As soon as we have become intimate and have entered the personal, private space of the other person, we have created a familiarity; a familiarity that, if we are not careful, can lead to disrespect and a dishonouring of ourselves if we do not continue filling that space with spiritual power and wisdom. After

27

the honeymoon is over the comfort zone of such relationships can feel more like a *dis*comfort zone. Love can become an obligation, rather than an act of selflessness. It is then a little too late, for we have already set in motion the cycle of action and reaction.

Trying then to remove that person from your internal world can take a lifetime, especially if feelings of resentment have developed. When the other person has penetrated so deeply into your life, you may feel they have trapped you from the inside. But take a reality check: have they trapped you or are you still holding on? Freedom need only be one thought away.

As your self-worth increases the past will automatically drop away with ease, because you realize that you and your internal assets are too important. Boost your self-worth by respecting your time, thoughts, feelings, energy and other resources and don't give others the leeway to take advantage. Remember, you are the master of your personal treasures.

It's a paradox, but one important way toward a freer spirit, is for you to set clear boundaries on how far someone can enter your personal space and inner world. Remember that it's you who is giving them the permission to enter. Although boundaries may also sound like bondage, they are actually there for your protection. For example, when you fasten your seat belt you feel the pressure of it against your chest, but somehow know you are safer and calmer for it being there.

Real freedom is when we are able to do the things we want to do without anyone, or anything, infringing on that, and also not being forced into doing anything we don't want to do.

It is the mind that we need to set free. Sometimes it can be stubborn, and at other times delusional and easily persuaded. Sometimes attachment can justify its existence: 'Oh, but these people need me'. Sometimes, ego rationalizes its position: 'I need the degree in order to get things moving around here'. Greed will also raise its head and make excuses: 'But my health will deteriorate without these comforts and lifestyle'. The more we free ourselves from these frills and trappings, the lighter and freer the soul will feel.

IT'S TIME... to realize that as you begin to experience freedom from your inner negativity, insecurities and dependencies, you become the agent of true and lasting freedom. You hold the key to your inner world, so learn to discern carefully who should enter it. If you feel trapped, ask yourself: what am I clinging on to? A truly free spirit holds on to nothing: it is this lightness that makes it fly so easily.

Soul mate

Our society continues to pay a huge price for the myth of romantic love. It's a tempting notion that somewhere out there is our soul mate, a Mr or Ms Right who will complete us and that the feelings of loneliness, hollowness, meaninglessness, boredom and unworthiness will melt away with this union. We long to be in the warm affectionate arms of an adoring partner who will understand us and know the depth, wonder and secret of our being. Poets speak of this promise with their eloquent tongues. A succession of broken hearts and marriages may crack this notion for many, but for most the dream continues.

Pick up just about any magazine these days and you'll find numerous articles on how to improve relationships or to find true love. If everyone has been searching so long for true love, and the magazines can provide all the answers, why do so many people still feel lonely and dissatisfied, even after finding their 'other half'? It seems that the extent to which we analyze and idealize the issue of loving relationships is in direct proportion to how far we have moved away from exactly what it is we are searching for. In the name of love we give away a lot of our inner power.

The pretty picture of fulfilment painted on the canvas of our mind is really of a deeper union we seek with our inner self. When was the last time you made an appointment to spend quality time with yourself? As we move away from our authentic self we begin to project our needs onto someone out there who is also doing the same thing, and in that moment we set ourselves up for disappointment, no matter how genuine the other party may be. The qualities we are attracted to in another are those which we lack within ourselves. This lack creates the feeling of emptiness. To achieve genuine fulfilment we have to do the inner work of getting to know ourselves and filling in those missing qualities. Only then can our relationships with others be based on equality and sharing, rather than needing and wanting.

It is a fortunate soul who understands that the more love they have for themselves, the more they can bring to any relationship. That individual will automatically have self-esteem and will have dealt with a lot of their own emotional baggage that is so poisonous to relationships. It's from a place of fullness and genuine inner love – the pure heart – that we are truly able to give and share without dependency and expectation. If we give love from this place of fullness, then we will most certainly experience the return of it.

Imagine if each of us were to act from a place of fullness. The world would certainly be a different place. We would no longer need to use the expression 'falling' in love, as we would know that in true love, we can only 'rise'.

Spiritual love does not weigh or measure, log or document. It does not worship or adore another. Spiritual love is infinite, impartial and trusting. It is available in absolute abundance.

IT'S TIME... to befriend yourself. This is the time to 'rise in love' and to reclaim your own inner power and beauty and to become whole once again. The whole world will thank you and you will rejoice in having found your true and perfect soul mate.

Breaking down the inner fort

The image of the fortress has always been fascinating. Built to withstand any attack from hostile forces, it represented a place of safety and shelter; a wall of protection from enemies and a show of strength. Sometimes we can build internal walls that serve a similar function, but in the illusion of creating a place of protection for ourselves, how much are we in fact imprisoning our 'self' instead?

Whether the fortress is built outside or within ourselves, there is no protection in dense walls; there is only protection in virtue. When one is full of virtue, always giving happiness and accumulating an account of good deeds, one no longer needs the protection of walls. Our conscience is clear and there is no longer any need to fear.

As scared and weak individuals, we often begin construction of our own inner fortress early in life to protect ourselves from disappointments, unfulfilled dreams and from people who may hurt us. As we get older our accumulated negative experiences often serve to fortify these walls and make them stronger and even more impenetrable. In the attempt to keep ourselves safe we prevent ourselves from receiving love, cooperation and good wishes from others.

For those who have thickened the walls of their inner fortress, time may crack them, allowing the light to come in, and with it, other people too. The process of simply being aware awakens us to the freedom beyond the wall, beyond our fears, our hurts and our false ego. It reveals how the wall shields us less than it traps and separates us. The energy we expend to

fortify the wall is energy taken away from exploring our inner strengths, from learning the beauty in being, from experiencing the wonder of life, and from enjoying the warmth of the light; the light that comes from our true self-respect.

With spiritual power, we can come to know that there is a better way to live and we can succeed in breaking down those walls and barriers, little by little, brick by brick. To let others in we have to manage our own expectations first. Over time and with a little compassion, we can replace the barrier to our hearts with trust, faith and an inner sense of being able to take care of ourselves.

There is victory for those who have the courage to break down their inner walls. They have the opportunity to become flexible, more able to accept change, and they develop a new ability to embrace the beauty of life. They are able to manage the ups and downs that life brings them. Their capacity to love and be loved expands. They have a very good sense of who they are and what they stand for and are open to any challenge in life. The world is no longer their enemy and there is no threat to be feared.

When an enemy appears to threaten and oppose you and seems to block your vision and your path you begin to feel defenceless and fearful, and you may feel that your only options are 'fight or flight'. However, in the light of meditation one sees the truth, which is that the enemy is not out there. The real foe is not on the other side of the wall, but right here within us. Thus, we are only fighting with ourselves or running from ourselves, in other words, we are fighting inside our own fort.

Fortresses are indeed a thing of the past. They served a purpose in their times, but now they are relics of our history. So too, make your inner fortress a thing of the past. Use meditation as the tool with which to break down your walls, brick by brick, and replace them with an aura of light and love. Instead of a wall of fear, create a flow of energy that allows your real powers and strengths to emerge and also invites others to step in and experience the light.

IT'S TIME... to check your level of self-respect and self-trust. Be courageous, begin to be more open and accepting and see how many bricks are removed to let light into your soul. Check to see what threatens your freedom. Ask yourself "Why?" or "How?" this is happening. Use your inner powers and strengths, your thoughts, words and your spiritual love, for these are your true circle of protection.

No man (or woman) is an island

No Man is an Island is a famous book penned by the English writer John Donne in 1624. Whilst Donne recovered from a serious illness he wrote a series of reflections on life. It is unfortunate that we have such divine revelations when we are in our sickbed, when we have more need of them when we are on the rollercoaster of life. This statement is as valid today as it was in the 17th century.

Many of us take pride in our independence, whether it is our ability to walk on our own or to make our way alone in the world. This level of individual success deserves to be acknowledged, but does it define us? Does independence mean I am a sovereign island unto myself?

If we hold on to our independence too tightly we will not be able to give of our self. More importantly, we will lose opportunities to share other people's talents and abilities – to create something greater than our self. Independence should not take away from the greater goal of unity.

When we engage, express and exchange, it is then that we feel inter-connected. We feel a purpose for living as we realize our life is not just for ourselves alone, but for sharing and caring. Imagine a world where each one of us went about our lives having no contact whatsoever with another living soul. No touch, speech or eye contact; each person living in isolation and only being concerned or preoccupied with themselves. Would life be worth living?

It is one of life's ironies that many people who live alone leave the TV buzzing all day, just to hear some voices in the house. Or they leave the windows open, just to be able to hear some sounds from the outside world. They want their own space, yet just enough connection with the bigger world to confirm they are still alive.

The concept that no man is an island is further explored by fiction writer Frigyes Karinthy. He was the first proponent of the 'six degrees of separation' concept, in his 1929 short story, *Chains*. 'Six degrees of separation' is the idea that a maximum of five intermediaries are required to connect two people in a chain of 'a friend of a friend' statement.

Subsequent empirical studies have revealed that in some social structures, three degrees of separation exist even within very large populations such as the U.S.

Whatever the quantitative measurement, there is a common element that creates a subtle link between every one of us. In fact, we are intricately connected in a human web and the quality of our closeness will determine the value of our relationships.

As life gets more complex, the importance of support increases. Advances in science have also helped us conclude that a species is likely to survive and thrive if they are cooperative, communicative, connected and mutually supportive. It has been consistently demonstrated that people with a strong support network and sense of community live longer, are less vulnerable to illness, and tend to live happier and more fulfilled lives. What we are able to achieve collectively as a family, society, or country is greater than the individual can achieve alone.

Globalization, which is driven by a combination of economic, technological, socio-cultural and political factors, has demonstrated the importance of being more integrated. The term also refers to the transnational circulation of ideas, languages, or popular culture through acculturation. One nation's success, excellence, advancement, discovery, development or innovation can help another if they so choose.

But sadly, due to greed, we live in a world where everyone wants monopoly over what they invent. In fact, the world was not created with borders and boundaries that seem so clear and sharp on the world map. It is our ego and attachments that have created separation and a false sense of being self-sufficient.

There is a saying that a butterfly flapping its wings in Africa has a ripple effect in causing storms in Alaska. We all affect each other with our decisions and actions. Nations are not isolated and cannot consider themselves as independent states, no matter how rich and powerful they think they are.

We rudely pollute our skies and oceans, take voraciously from Mother Earth, consume excessively without recycling and expect the world to continue providing the same quality harvest. Is it practical or possible? Does everything not have a limit?

Some mega corporations are taking social responsibility and aim to give back to the earth what they have taken, but it is the responsibility of each individual to help replenish the world. With all our diminishing resources, it is imperative that humanity learns its lesson and starts to cooperate and collaborate with all members of this planet before it is too late to do so.

Spirituality means to collaborate and cooperate. There are no enemies and no discrimination, only pure love for one another throughout the world. This may seem like a dream but deep within every soul there is a desire for such a world. The truth of the matter is we cannot want that which we have not experienced.

We primarily isolate ourselves from others when we lack tolerance; we often expect to receive first, rather than to give. However, as meditators, the more we are at peace on our own inner island, the more happiness we generate and hence feel confident in being with others. We learn to make our mind our own best friend before trying to make others our best friend.

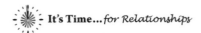 **It's Time...** *for Relationships*

IT'S TIME... to remember that just as you value your independence, those who are truly independent cooperate, communicate and connect with others in the world. They appreciate those from whom they take support, and care for those who need their support. Remember that this whole world is one big island that we all share. If we could remove all the boundaries and limitations in the world, then there would be nothing we have to cross.

Part Two...

Our relationships
with others

Emotional proximity

Why is it that with some people we can let down our guard and feel totally comfortable and yet with others the walls just won't yield. With some we can eat from the same plate and sip from the same cup, whilst others we keep at arm's length.

It is a common belief that North Americans need three feet of space between them when conversing and yet South Americans, or those from warmer climates, require only a few inches of personal space. What defines our level of comfort and proximity?

The act of falling in love is also an act of letting down our guard, allowing the other person to enter our mind and heart and then our whole life, until there is no sense of separateness. This is often thought of as being one soul in two bodies.

Have you ever wondered why it is, that in anger we have to shout and in love we only need to whisper? If the physical proximity is the same, what is the difference? It is love and an open heart.

Our physical, and more importantly, emotional proximity is often determined by how willing and open we are to listening to and understanding the other person; to care for and share with others. For example, stepping into a room filled with ten people can feel overwhelming if you don't know them, but if all are friends or relatives, then ten can seem such a small number.

To feel the need for physical space is more about needing mental space where there is not the meeting of minds. When one feels safe, accepted and loved, then there is no need to put up any fences. Most of our defences are a form of self-defence.

In our vulnerability we are unsure of how we will be accepted, so we protect ourselves by being polite and quiet, disengaging, and by staying away.

Ultimately, how close we feel to somebody will be in relation to how close we feel to ourselves. We deny ourselves the right to engage because of many of our own emotions, such as fear, sensitivity and pain. If we are secure in our truth then we do not need to protect ourselves and to battle; we can give freely from the heart. If our heart is full then we can let go of the fear that someone might hurt us. In reality, it is our own reactions to the behaviour of others that causes pain. If we come from a place of bigheartedness then we will be too busy giving to take sorrow from any situation. Therefore, no defence is necessary.

To create a one-world family we need to open our hearts and minds and to embrace everyone. We need to be less judgmental and more accepting. If we are to create a world in which there are no barriers, then we need to firstly make friends with ourselves and then do what comes naturally: Be love. Give love.

IT'S TIME... to recognize that the walls you have built around you will not protect you but only serve to isolate and to trap you. Letting go of them can open you up to a whole new world of possibilities.

Give and ye shall receive

For our own peace of mind when we give it should be with a pure heart. When we give with strings attached neither the giver nor receiver stays happy forever. When we give conditionally it spoils the relationship, even though our intentions may have been coming from the right place.

If mother knits Bobby a jumper and expects him to wear it once a week he will possibly resent her and wish he never took the sweater in the first place. If Kenny gives Kyle a new iPhone is it not up to Kyle to do with it as he wishes? Whether he gives it to his younger brother, resells it or dumps it in the bin. Once a gift is given it no longer belongs to the giver. Both parties get hurt when the giving is loaded with expectations. It is our ego that feels the hurt at what appears to be a lack of gratitude. This tells us that our giving was really an attempt at taking. We gave because we wanted something in return.

What about birthday presents? Do you automatically assume you will receive a birthday present from the same person you have given one to? Perhaps you feel annoyed when you realize that their present didn't match the monetary value of the one you gave them.

Giving, and then waiting in anticipation of a return in kind, or in the form of thanks or acknowledgement, only makes us into beggars. When we give, let it be from a place of abundance and generosity. Think of the kings in bygone times who had treasure troves of wealth. Those kings had ample wealth and their stock was never depleted. Therefore, be a king and not a beggar. Go beyond to the kingdom of the soul. When the soul

was abundant and bountiful the only thing it knew was how to give without a thought of taking. Now go beyond and tap into your inner resources; to the kingdom of the soul.

In addition to expecting gratitude or more in return for our giving, we brag about what we have given up, or we complain about what we had to forgo. We tell our children how we gave up opportunities just to bring them up. We moan to our spouse about not having enough time to do certain wonderful things because we are too busy being the breadwinner. It is best to keep well away from this kind of sacrifice talk; being a martyr does not endear us to anyone. This is emotional blackmail and in these situations no one ends up happy. Be mature and do things out of choice and not under duress or to please people. Allow others to appreciate what you are doing without trying to make them feel indebted to you.

Today one of the reasons for divorce is that one party thinks they are pulling more weight than the other. For sure, communication is important to bring balance, but more importantly, do things because you want to do them. When the sharing or caring is not done with pure intent we end up hurting ourselves and that distress spills over into relationships as bitterness. When we have given, or given up something through self-sacrifice, then let it be from the heart.

A soul who has self-respect also has good self-esteem and is less needy and dependent on another individual dealing with similar emotional issues. It is from the spiritual heart, from fullness and inner love that we are truly able to give and share with each other. The more plentiful we feel inside, the less we need from outside sources. Imagine a world of givers, not takers.

Remember that the saying is 'give and ye shall receive', not 'receive and ye shall give'. In other words, give of what you have and you will inevitably receive. Don't wait to receive before you give. The law of 'sow and reap' demands that we pay in advance. We first have to give to the earth before it can reward us with a harvest. We know that if our karma, actions, are good, the fruit that results from the seeds of our best intentions will bear the best fruit.

In wounded relationships, forgiveness is the key. To do this, we first need to replenish ourselves and replace what we gave out. We think forgiveness is about the other person, but in truth it all begins with yourself.

Don't get tired of giving from the heart. Our sole purpose is to give. Mother Nature gives constantly and it is also our nature to do the same. Mother Nature gives from the heart, knowing that abundance is the natural law. Contrary to what we might think, when we give from the heart, that place within where there is already abundance, then we do not become empty.

Giving should fulfil us, not deplete us. There is more joy in giving than receiving. As we give, we know we will receive and so there is no fear of losing anything. It is those with empty hearts who don't give and are therefore left feeling empty and fearful, for they have not participated in the natural flow of life; that of giving and receiving. So, remember the basic principle of give and take is that you get back what you give out.

IT'S TIME... to give just for the pure joy of giving. Give because you want to give. Don't boast about all the big sacrifices you made or are currently making. Don't make the other party feel guilty; you have a choice, exercise it. Make sure your giving is not an exchange as with those birthday presents, give from the heart and don't expect anything in return. Once you have begun this process watch out for the avalanche, as you may receive more than you can handle.

It drives me nuts when...

Many of us are excellent at pointing the finger at others and finding fault with what we think is not working. But are we as good at pointing the finger at ourselves?

Next time you find yourself criticising something or complaining about others, finish the rest of this statement: "It drives me nuts when..." and write down all the annoying things this person does.

For example: "It drives me nuts when this person doesn't put things back in their place." Or, "It drives me nuts when they are too slow in finishing their sentences." Or, "It drives me nuts when this person is late to our meeting."

When you dare take a deeper look, you will most likely find that those are the exact same things you don't like about yourself.

These issues may be projections onto others, or simply an area of life in which you are trying to improve upon in yourself and not quite succeeding. Because how else would you recognise it? These triggers provide tons of information about what is going on in the soul, which is where the deepest change needs to take place and not out there on the outside.

IT'S TIME... to share a moment of compassion, knowing that you could also be guilty of that which you despise. Love moves mountains, so love yourself and begin to move your inner mountain and you will see the scenery automatically change.

Don't just expect, reflect

We live in an imperfect world and yet we expect our relationships to be perfect. We want almost everyone to be flawless: friends, family, colleagues, bus drivers and traffic attendants. But it's a tall order to ask for, isn't it? We conveniently forget that we ourselves are not perfect. Overcoming our ego and accepting others 'warts and all' is a big part of living in harmony. Trying to change others will not bring harmony.

We often expect that when we agree to do something with someone it should happen like clockwork. This does not always happen. Hope for the best but expect to be ready to change gear at any moment. The less we demand of others, the more friction-free and happier our relationships will become.

People are intuitive and can pick up when we are trying to change them, control them, or fix them. We love people, but at the same time we love moulding them as if they were clay and believe that perhaps a slight comment here, a remark there and a joke made 'in jest', will pull them into shape. Anyone sensing that you are out to change them will resist and most likely run in the opposite direction.

Weigh your words. Words spoken out of line are hard to retrieve and difficult to repair. Sometimes it's better to be a little tolerant and patient and fix ourselves first, rather than spoil our relationships with incessant demands. It's really not worth having everything perfect if it's at the cost of sacrificing valuable relationships.

If you look for people's weaknesses you will very often find them. No one is perfect; all of us are fallible. Your best mate may

be a saint at times, but at some point he or she will surely let you down, and most likely when you need them the most. This is one of life's lessons. It teaches us that life is a game of give and take. It teaches us to be compassionate, humble, kind hearted and not to put demands or expectations on others.

It's so easy to see the defects and weaknesses of others. We don't even have to look for them because we have trained ourselves to notice the negative before the positive. And so they make their presence known like thorns: pricking, prodding, causing pain and stating 'here I am!' But if we try to see it another way we may just realize that the weaknesses of others hurt us because we're still healing from a previous wound and we have not built immunity in that area yet.

For example, if I am hurt by what others say then I can check to see if I have set myself up for this heartache. Have my ears been waiting in anticipation for the sweet music of praise, adoration, or appreciation to float my way, and I have felt disappointed when the orchestra doesn't play to my tune? If my ego is hurt, it's because I have an ego. No one has hurt me; I have hurt myself by allowing the words to affect me. I have interpreted their meaning through my lens of vulnerability, judgment and expectation.

When we give attention and energy to someone's negative traits, they won't disappoint you; they will continue doing the exact thing that upsets you because your attention is the fuel they need to keep going. In fact, it will feel as if they have made it their occupation just to bug you.

Be prepared for surprises. Exercising an attitude of curiosity and acceptance rather than judgment can peel away layers in a relationship, softening and deepening them. Be fascinated by the differences, not put off. Trying to find out what compels someone to do something a certain way is a much better approach to repair a misunderstanding than to reprimand someone for not doing it. Or for that matter shouting because of the way it was done. Understand that everyone's style is different; remember there is always more than one way to do something and it is not necessarily your way.

We all have another side to us, it just depends if we bother to zoom in on it or not. Virtues in others may take a few minutes to notice but they are there, waiting to be spotted and adopted. In every area of life when you can find things in common with someone, you are better able to cooperate and collaborate. Mega corporations are harmonizing their energies with other mega corporations whose values approximate to their own and so there is no reason why you and I cannot.

IT'S TIME... to let go of your expectations of others and reflect on what matters most. There is no harm in hoping for others to be their best, but the moment you feel pain you have to ask: "Do I want the best for them or just for me?" Don't be too quick to judge; try to understand what makes others tick. The more you learn to let go of your expectations, the more life will surprise you in a good way.

Learning to say 'no'

When we are on a spiritual path it's important to affirm the positive whenever possible. However, on occasions it's important to learn to say 'no' in order to maintain healthy relationships. Therefore, we should not commit to saying 'yes' when, on the inside, feelings of resentment are brewing. Silence can also be seen as consent, so we need to communicate our needs clearly to those around us to avoid feelings of frustration and bitterness.

Saying 'no' can be especially difficult in intimate relationships. These are the relationships where all boundaries have been broken and there is often an unspoken contract that states: 'What is yours is mine and what is mine is yours.' Sometimes this is taken even further when the unspoken contract becomes: 'I have all rights over what you own, and so there is no need to ask or consult you for what is yours.'

Have you ever been in a situation where you felt obliged to lend your car to someone, but your intuition and inner voice were just not in favour of it? Perhaps you had loaned the person your car in the past, out of generosity of your heart, but then noticed that every time they brought it back it was always dirty and had an empty tank.

So if you agreed once again to their request, despite your unwillingness, what urged you to say it? Was it to avoid hurt or bad feelings? Or was it to look good, generous and powerful in the eyes of the other? Was it out of weakness perhaps, or fear of their reactions? Or, to keep the peace, you simply gave in to your inner battle of 'yes – no', 'yes – no'?

When there is a struggle between the head wanting to say 'no' and the heart wanting to say 'yes' then one needs to really look within. Meditation is a tool that helps us to bring the head and the heart together, so that our thoughts, words and deeds are all in alignment. When there is this configuration one is at peace with oneself.

Meditation is about exploring the self and generating true self-respect and self-esteem. It's about being authentic in our thoughts, words and deeds so there is no pretence. Meditation gives us the power to stand up for our truth and if we do it with pure intentions, the truth is palatable when shared with all.

Every time we do something against our inner voice, in other words, when we say 'yes' when we really mean to say 'no', we kill a part of us from within. We lose honour and self-respect and resentment builds toward those we feel are forcing us into such corners.

By maintaining our self-respect, which also includes respect for our time, possessions, relationships and natural resources, as well as our mental and physical energies, then we are able to be assertive. We are able to say 'no' from a place of respect and not selfishness.

But, we need to learn to tread the fine line between being assertive and being passive or aggressive. To be assertive has to come from a place of higher self-respect. When we are in assertive mode we can respect ourselves and the other person at the same time. When we are passive or aggressive then we are being selfish and not respectful of either ourselves, or of others. In this situation we hand over our power to others, which weakens us. We can be assertive when we know clearly what we want and why we want it. If we are not clear then we will most likely be aggressive in our behaviour. By contrast, when we are in a passive state we may often ignore our own needs.

So, to use the car example again, what you are really seeking is respect for your possessions and yourself. When you don't get respect you feel hurt. Therefore, with high self-esteem, be polite and assertive. Don't feel embarrassed to let the other person know that they need to fill the gas tank. When words are spoken from a place of both self-respect and respect for the other party they will be heard and not resented.

Of course, good tone and positive body language, together with good feelings, are very important in communicating the message. Once the other party recognises that you are genuine and sincere they will oblige. This principle applies to everything we do. If we are shy to state our needs it is often us that gets hurt, while the other has enjoyed the pleasure and moved on happily.

There may be times when we need to say 'yes'. For example, it's often difficult to say 'no' to close family members where there is pressure to help each other out in times of need, and at any cost. This is OK as long as we don't 'lose ourselves' and develop ill feelings toward the other person in the process. So, in these cases we need to carefully reflect on the situation and then, if we agree and say 'yes', we can choose to do it with good feelings, dignity and grace.

IT'S TIME... to be authentic. Work on building your self-respect and state your needs carefully without hurting others. In doing this, everyone benefits and others will happily go the extra mile to help.

Lust is rust

Traditionally thought of as one of the seven deadly sins and therefore something to be approached with caution, lust is undeniably one of the most prevalent and pervasive influences in society today.

It's something we can hardly avoid facing at every turn, with every magazine page and every billboard. Yet, at the same time, it is a topic that is little understood. In reality, we are confused by this so-called sin that appears to promise the fulfilment of our dreams. If the satisfaction of our worldly desires is the key to happiness, then why is a liberal society not constantly experiencing a state of constant happiness, instead of the sad state that is the reality?

Lust is a yearning, a hunger of an emotional kind that never seems to be satisfied. Lust can exist for food, objects, status and fame. It holds people in its grip with endless temptation and a promise that fulfilment can only come from something outside of you, and that having more is better.

The mind is so intensely pulled in the direction of the object of desire that it seems impossible to be at peace until one has possessed, owned, experienced, or tasted it. But fulfilment of this kind is almost always temporary and limited. It leaves us with a gaping hole that expands continually and can never be filled. Any desire based on lust, greed, ego or attachment will only ever be fulfilled momentarily, for the next desire is always just around the corner.

Lust pollutes the mind and does not allow room for peace or clarity. Have you ever wondered where the term 'bachelor's degree' came from? Originally, studies were meant to be undertaken in a state of bachelorhood, where the person was single and free and their mind was not distracted by love or lust. Someone who is on a spiritual path understands that when we are at the mercy of our desires we cannot be in control of the self. When we learn to manage our senses we once again take control and regain mastery over our mind and body.

Another confusion in our minds is that lust and love are the same thing, or at least closely connected. However, the opposite is true. The hormones released when the mind is in a state of love promote healing and a sense of care and nurturing, whereas those released in the act of lovemaking are the same as those when a person is under attack. Can violence and love really coexist?

Our need for love is natural and important but it should not be confused with lust. For example, the love between a mother and her child is invaluable in the growth and development of the child. Yet, as adults we may think that if we are getting physical attention then we are being loved. This mistaken thinking can only lead to disappointment and sorrow.

In many faiths there is the notion of practising a period of abstention from desires, such as fasting and celibacy. This is a time to refrain from worldly and sensuous attractions and to turn the mind totally to the Divine. During Haj (pilgrimage), Muslims must abstain from sexual lust and impure thoughts. Hindus must abstain from sexual lust during the holy month of Shravan. In Christianity, priests and nuns also renounce the worldly pleasures of lust as a mark of their exclusive commitment to the Divine.

Thus, it is understood that the function of procreation belongs in its proper place. When it becomes recreation and we no longer have control over our bodily desires, we lose the ability to connect with higher, subtle energies. When the root, or sex, chakra that governs sexual energy is imbalanced, then our thoughts and actions primarily revolve around material possessions and security, over indulgence in sensual pleasures, violence and aggression, worry and uncertainty. Some forms of physical yoga focus on raising the energies to the higher chakras with the ultimate aim of connecting with the Divine through the crown chakra. When the mind is occupied by lust, the energies are base and it is like rust on the soul. It pulls us down to mundane matters and does not allow us to be lifted up by the One above.

Abstinence is not purely a religious or a moral concept. Nowadays there are more and more people choosing to live celibate lives even within a relationship, as harmony and respect is created and a sense of self-worth returns. In a healthy, pure relationship, real, unselfish love comes automatically.

With increasing incidences of rape, paedophilia and sex addiction in society today, it makes one wonder at the lengths to which individuals will go to experience love and belonging. For it is the quest to experience these states that is the real reason behind any desires however corrupted the action might be. It is a longing for connection at the deepest level and to experience a state of bliss, however temporary. As we move further away from spiritual fulfilment we apparently need to indulge more and more in this physical substitute. Ironically, this increasingly distances us from real fulfilment.

So this obsession with lust, be it for food, objects or another person, is the rust that prevents the soul from shining. It prevents us from experiencing deep inner peace, love, belonging and spiritual satisfaction, and it takes us away from the only connection that can truly fulfil all of our desires.

IT'S TIME... to realize that through the power of meditation we are indeed already full and complete. No object or person can give you the satisfaction that you are seeking inside. And as you clean yourself from all impure thoughts and desires, the

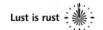

rust falls away and you will be automatically attracted to the Divine, who is a reflection of our higher, perfect state.

Overcoming codependency

Codependency is a sickness; it's an unhealthy love. Codependents generally have good intentions but low self-esteem and go looking for something outside themselves to make them feel better. The consequences of maintaining a codependent approach to life are often resentment, frustration and unmet personal needs.

Codependents try to take care of people, but the caretaking becomes compulsive and defeating. They project the illusion that they are caring, when in reality it is the act of keeping others dependent on them that fulfils their needs. They find it hard to be themselves. Some codependents seek solace through alcohol, drugs and nicotine, while others develop compulsive behaviours such as workaholism, gambling or indiscriminate sexual activity.

Codependency can occur in any type of relationship, including families, at work, in friendships and romantic relationships. It often involves putting one's needs at a lower priority than those of others, while being excessively preoccupied with fulfilling the needs of others. When codependents place other people's health, welfare and safety above their own they lose contact with their own needs, desires, and sense of self. This false sense of reward and satisfaction from being needed further traps the codependent in the relationship.

Mental Health America states:

> "Codependents often take on a martyr's role and become 'benefactors' to an individual in need. A wife may cover for her alcoholic husband; a mother may

make excuses for a truant child; or a father may 'pull some strings' to keep his child from suffering the consequences of delinquent behaviour." [1]

The important lesson to learn from any type of dependency, be it drugs, food or relationships, is that as soon as that 'drug' wears off, you will want more and more each time. If that's not possible then we may revert to anger and different forms of emotional manipulation to get what we think we need.

Need and greed can often be confused. We live in the illusion that 'more' is satisfying or gratifying, when in actual fact it reinforces the habit of dependency and slavery and, in some cases, death.

Research shows that:

> "People with codependency are also more likely to attract further abuse from aggressive individuals, more likely to stay in stressful jobs or relationships, less likely to seek medical attention when needed and are less likely to get promotions and tend to earn less money than those without codependency patterns." [2]

Dependency almost always begins with the way we think. Some people just can't have a good day until they have had their bout of complaining and grouching. They like to begin their day with their morning coffee and a dose of negative thoughts. Others are addicted to the Cinderella complex – 'Poor me!' And they go around thinking they are the victims and the world revolves around them. This mindset doesn't serve anyone.

Hence, every spiritual path advocates surrendering or abandoning addictions. They distract us from our real pursuit of transcendental peace and bliss. They hold us tightly within

---

1   See *Mental Health America, Codependency, http://mentalhealthamerica.net/go/codependency,* 13 September 2012.
2   See *Wikipedia, Codependency, http://en.wikipedia.org/wiki/Codependency,.* 13 September 2012

the reins of an illusion that pain will be assuaged or feelings of deprivation will be satiated some day. We just keep hoping and praying.

The feelings of deprivation or emptiness drive us to go looking for that secret elixir. Much of the lack is more in our mind than in our life. The pursuit of happiness will not be met by being propped up from outside, but through a closer connection with our inner self.

The first step is to acknowledge the damage this dependency is having on our relationships, health and finances. Ask yourself: 'Is this how I am choosing to live my life?' With more difficult issues such as drugs, professional help may be needed, together with intense work on rebuilding self-respect and a sense of deserving better in life.

The second step is to be reflective and acknowledge that everything we need is right here, right now, inside us. We need nothing extra to complete ourselves. When we look for completion from outside ourselves, we attempt to hold so tightly onto our object of desire that we only succeed in suffocating it or driving it away.

The third step is to be cautious not to create more negative karma with the people around us. If we help fuel the addictions of others, then we are a shareholder in their negative karma.

Finally, if we are to be dependent, then let us be dependent on God. He is the one Being who will never let us down. He is always giving and ready to empower us.

IT'S TIME... to reflect on your dependencies. By changing patterns of thinking and increasing your self-worth you will be self-contained and take inner strength from your close relationship with God. Independence does not mean to be isolated or alone, but means choosing to not take pain ever again from relationships.

The power to tolerate

With the increasingly rapid changes in society today, there has never been as great a need as there is now to exercise tolerance.

Religious tolerance, cultural tolerance, tolerance toward the weather, to globalization, to wealth inequality, the list is endless. What about those small events at home or in the office that 'press our buttons'? The unemptied dishwasher, that dirty tea cup left by your colleague, or the water cooler humming away as you try to meditate. Anything and everything can become a reason to create havoc in the mind if one has not mastered the power of tolerance.

To tolerate sounds like a tedious and tiresome task. The term has been degraded over time to imply a struggle, suffering, or a battle to be endured. Some believe that to tolerate means to become a doormat, but this is far from the case when we develop accurate tolerance.

The power to tolerate means to remain seated in self-respect and not to give power away to a situation or to a person, thereby hurting oneself. It's about being a master and choosing an appropriate peaceful response, rather than being a slave who is pushed and pulled around by circumstances, feeling agonised and out of control.

It's therefore logical to say that it is not the situation itself that is the problem, but rather one's inability to deal with it that creates a feeling of weakness or intolerance. For example, the sound of the ticking clock is not the real problem for the yogi, but the inability to shut out the sound that creates the negative, uncomfortable feelings of intolerance. Similarly, we cannot

63

blame language or dialect when our communication with others breaks down. Perhaps it's our lack of patience?

One who has mastered the power of tolerance presides over the situation and will not create extra unnecessary thoughts about the person who might be messy, or the event which may be delayed, or the thing like the car breaking down. Instead, he will be the detached observer, not caught up in fixing things, but accepting the flow of the drama of life and the roles of all the fellow actors. To want to change something in the drama of life means to change the master script, and that key is only in the hands of the Divine.

The yogi, as a master, knows to be free from expectation and judgement; nothing is right or wrong, it just is. So accept what 'is' first of all, and then move on from there. It's not all about being passive. Yes, we may have to take some corrective action, but if this is done from a place of tolerance and love it will be much more effective than anger and condemnation.

As the master learns to stay silent, he is also freeing himself from his ego and his karmic debts. To shout as a reaction to someone's bitter words will only intensify the bondage of karma. To step back, instead of jumping out at someone, takes courage and self-respect.

To take it one step further, the master will see but not see, hear but not hear; he will be in a state of equanimity and be indifferent. That is when he knows he is 'beyond'. The yogi understands that the drama of life is perfect; he is at complete peace, in complete calm and his responses will be ones of compassion, understanding and love, even in the face of criticism. Much like the tolerant mother who continues to forgive and give to her children.

IT'S TIME... to disengage from your ego and take a good look at yourself, knowing that the solution to your own intolerance lies within you. If you care enough for your self then it's time

64

to develop compassion and self-respect. Cultivate more peace within and peace with others. That way you won't even feel that you are tolerating, but that life is a game and, whilst playing, you will always have fun.

The law of sow and reap

The law that states 'As you sow, so shall you reap' can be found in almost every holy book. In science, it's often referred to as the 'law of cause and effect', in philosophy as the 'law of karma' and Newton's third law of motion is, 'For every action there is an equal and opposite reaction'. So, it's important to remember that this principle affects every area of our lives.

In each moment we are presented with a choice. We can choose good over evil, be kind or be rude, move slow or fast, make things simple or complicated, and so on. Depending on what action we take, we receive the return of that. It's that simple. Do good and you get something good in return. Give love and you are showered with love.

We can only get back what we give out. If we plant tomatoes, we can't expect pumpkins. If we are managing our weight, it's because we exercise and regulate our diet. If we have a successful career, it's probably due to years of hard work and continuous effort. If we are enjoying warm loving friendships today, then that's because we have tilled the ground of our relationships.

The life we live today is the consequence of our previous actions. Even though it may feel as if it's taken a long time to get to where we are, and we can't wait to receive the return, it's only a matter of patience because all seeds yield fruit in their own time.

The same is true for the adverse. If we criticize others, we will be criticized. If we steal, we will be robbed. If we lie and cheat, we will be lied to and cheated. But it may not always come back to us in the same way. For example, if we cheat in business, perhaps our husband or wife will cheat on us at home.

But isn't it interesting that during these setbacks and losses it's not so easy to accept the outcome? We often have the audacity to question when things don't go as we wish: 'Why me?' 'How is this possible?' Funnily enough we don't question when things seem to go our way.

Should we only use the law of sow and reap to justify our present relationships and disposition, or should it be about choosing to create a brighter future, since the 'seeds' are in our own hands? The law is fair and just, it only requires that we pay in advance, for we cannot reap if we have not sown. We first have to give to the earth, even if it's with our last seed, before it can reward us with a bounty. Remember nature is very generous. When we plant one mango seed we don't just get one mango, we get many in return, and over several years.

We must remember that karma is the law of give and take, not take and give. We can only take when we have first given, even if it's our last seed, coin or object of love. If we take without having given, we have ignored the law and the consequence is we pay back multi-fold in order to return balance to the soul. When we take we create debt, and the ultimate aim is to remain free of debt and be in credit at all times. To achieve this we need to give more than we take. Let's examine this further:

Time
Time is a valuable asset, and we very often find that we do not have enough time. Each second that passes will never return. Yet, when we create a positive karma with time, we have ample time to do all the things we want to do; time cooperates with us. When we waste time, we have not utilized that time appropriately in fulfilling our own purpose, so we are punished with a shortage of time.

Wealth
Some people have plenty of wealth and yet carry around a needy and impoverished consciousness. Thus, it's not the wealth that

makes one wealthy, but the attitude of having it all even whilst having little. Wealth used for a higher purpose yields the greatest return, hence the importance given to charity for a worthy cause.

Mind and body

Our thoughts and energy are our most valuable resources. If we misuse them then we reap the consequences. If we think about useless and negative things we will probably get a headache. If we look at our TV screen all day we will probably need glasses. If we use our lungs to inhale nicotine instead of oxygen, then of course they will become unhappy and resentful and fail to function properly.

Nature

When we dispose of rubbish appropriately, or learn not to waste water and other natural resources, we create a relationship of love and respect with Mother Nature. It doesn't matter what everyone else throws out of their car window; our duty is to create our own personal relationship, our own personal account of respect with Nature and the five elements. Only then can nature help us when we are in need and make sure that we always have food, water and air when we need it.

Relationships

Some people seem to be connected to many others and yet when they need help very few people are around to return the favour. Relationships are an investment. The more we invest love, respect, kindness, cooperation and compassion in our relationships, the more we get in return.

IT'S TIME... to till the soil of your mind and remove the weeds of unwanted thoughts, feelings and undesired outcomes. You are the master of your mind and thus you can choose to create the results you seek. Plant wholesome seeds of positive and powerful thoughts in all areas of your life, not only in your relationships, and watch the fruits appear. But, be patient, for unripe fruit can cause indigestion.

Pure love

Many find it hard to understand the notion of pure love: most have never experienced it. Romantics believe jealousy and possessiveness are central elements of passionate love. Mothers feel attachment is necessary to show care and concern. Friends believe expectations are integral to friendship. Pure love is least understood and yet most desirable. So, let's take a deeper look at what exactly pure love is.

Pure love means to want nothing: nada, zilch. Sometimes we convince ourselves that we have the right to something from our partners, spouses or close ones, but we don't. To want makes us beggars and in reality the beggar does not deserve pure love, he deserves pure pity.

Pure love cannot be given; it can only be shared by two beings that share a pure and equal intent. When two individuals don't share the same pure love the quality of their exchange turns into a need for help, sympathy, comfort, approval, confirmation or security. The giver is forever filling a bottomless pit inside the taker, with so-called love.

Pure love does not expect anything. I may not want, but I will expect and the two are slightly different. For example, I may not want love, or perhaps feel full of it, yet I may still expect others to be loving toward me in some manner or form.

Although marriage is a contract, love is not. You cannot own someone or get someone to love you just because they have signed a contract to be with you 'For better or for worse till death do us part'. Pure love does not demand. Pure love is natural, gracious and freeing. It binds, but only to your higher, true, pure and perfect self.

The opposite of this freedom is that we create a relationship of 'Mr and Mrs Fix It'. To expect anything of another means to set myself up for disappointment as I realise that I cannot 'fix' anyone. I have to accept that I am the guilty party, not the other, for setting up false expectations in a world where more are empty, rather than full of pure love.

In pure love we are detached, meaning we are unaffected by the outcome. When we are detached from the outset we do not hold onto anything. We let go and accept the person or the situation with no preferences of like or dislike. This is a freeing thought for ourselves and for the ones we love. It allows newness, magic and mysticism to flow.

Having pure love means to bring others closer to themselves and to their inner truth; there is utmost honesty and a deep respect for the soul and the process. We may not see someone in their highest self today, but we know that tomorrow, if we continue with our generosity of pure love, they will ascend to their greatness. Therefore, wish the best for the one you love and not necessarily what is in *your* best interests.

Pure love means to keep the highest attitude and vision for every soul. We realize, through a vision of soul consciousness, how lovely each one is; it's not an effort to see this. Once we are set in our highest self-respect, it's easy to see everyone through this lens.

Be careful not to project your needs onto someone else. In a world where no one is emotionally complete, it's a tall order and impossible to fulfil. In pure love we do not demand. We trust. We trust that we will have the abundance we need and that the drama of life will deliver the right people and situations to help us feel the beauty of pure love.

God's love is the purest. He doesn't measure His love nor love you on Tuesdays and not Thursdays. His love is constant and truly altruistic. Although we can't be God, we can learn that divine love has to be of the same measure: pure, constant and selfless, first for the self and then for others.

IT'S TIME... to share love of the highest quality – pure love. Greatness lies in returning to this pure, divine consciousness. Stay detached from the offset and do not allow personal likes and dislikes to get in the way of the flow of the beautiful actors and the drama of life. Pure love is freeing and generous, embracing and rewarding. Sign this contract of pure love with your higher self.

Conflict management

Conflict is neither good or bad, it just 'is', and should be accepted as part of living in a global community. Depending on how conflict is managed it can be quite a healthy experience. It can teach us new skills and levels of understanding, it can build confidence and self-respect and it can release us from stagnation and lead us to a positive outcome. Conflict is about living with our differences, it's not a case of being right or wrong. At worst, one can always agree to disagree.

The word 'resolution' is derived from the Latin 're', which means once again and 'solvent' meaning no further distillation. Therefore, conflict resolution is about getting to the essence of what is causing the conflict.

The theory of martial arts can help us a lot when learning how to deal with our enemy. If we can embrace the conflict then we can use it to add to our own power and advantage. We can overthrow our opponent with our quick thinking, reflexes and flexibility, some of the keystrokes required in self-defence arts such as Aikido and Judo. Therefore, no matter how big and muscular the problem may seem, with the proper use of self-management skills we can tackle any hurdle.

There are some basic conflict management styles that people use to deal with their problems. Some accommodate to just be able to get along. Some avoid conflict altogether. Some compete and some compromise. Best of all would be to collaborate to find a mutually acceptable solution.

Stop for a minute to identify your style of conflict management. There is no right or wrong, all the styles serve their purpose and are appropriate in varying situations. It's important to know which one you are more inclined to use, so that you can pre-determine your response to conflict.

If we know what triggers us then that is half the problem. Most of the time the conflict is perceived in the mind. Imagine you work in an office. How many times have you expected your secretary to pick up the folders from your desk and file them away? Then at other times you don't want them to be touched, since you have neatly sorted them and will want to look at them the next day. You expect your secretary to be your mind reader and when this is not the case there is a conflict. These kinds of situations create a lot of unnecessary thoughts, which result in ill feelings and negative attitudes. We fall into the language of 'always' and 'never'. We are so frustrated that the people around us have not yet learnt the art of mind reading that we accuse them of 'always' disrupting our work, or 'never' doing anything around here.

This kind of attitude serves no purpose. A key element in conflict management is the need to communicate. Clear, effective communication is a must in order to avoid misunderstandings, fears, doubts and worries. Assumptions can never replace dialogue. When we express ourselves clearly it doesn't leave any margin for unnecessary or extra thoughts. So when the boss says, 'Please leave the files on the desk, I'll look at them tomorrow', the message is clear and both parties know what is expected.

Accurate conflict resolution is about getting to the bottom of issues that dominate the conflict situation. There's always more to the situation than meets the eye. Conflicts are synonymous with icebergs, as 90 percent of the iceberg is below the surface and only 10 percent is visible, just like us. In order to deal with conflicts we have to know who we are beneath the surface.

For example, if we are trying to apply the skill of active listening, which is based on the principle of respect for the point of view and feelings of others, yet inside we do not value or respect the other person, we will likely encounter discomfort within ourselves and not be able to resolve the conflict. Similarly, our attempt at using listening skills will sound and feel artificial – to ourselves as well as others. Therefore, new, genuine behaviours need to become part of how we think and feel.

Here are some conflict management skills you can try:

Clear communication
Don't leave any margin for assumption. Communicate your needs, wishes and desires in an effective and respectful manner.

Increase your inner work
Understanding oneself is a very deep subject and the lessons can last a lifetime. Reflect, and look inside yourself to assess what's going on before pointing the finger at others.

Weigh up the cost of the conflict
Before taking any step it's important to weigh up the cost of avoiding the conflict. If we are clear on our gains and losses it will give us a picture of how to proceed.

Build up your power base
The collaborative conflict resolution process is designed to use power to benefit both parties and is reflective of establishing an environment of mutual respect.

When speaking, talk from the 'I' perspective
'I' statements indicate you take responsibility for your thoughts, feelings and behaviour. People are less likely to object to 'I' statements. Stay away from blame and express what you see, hear, think or feel. For example, try saying: "I feel frustrated because I am not allowed to finish my sentences', rather than 'You keep

interrupting me all the time!" *Then* state what you need in clear, specific and positive terms. For example, "As I think it is important we both listen fully to each other, I would ask that we ensure each gets the chance to speak without interruption."

Move from judgment to curiosity

If we approach conflicts with an attitude of judgment about others or ourselves we will find it difficult to be collaborative. Judgmental thinking implies that one person is right and the other is wrong and creates a situation of 'you versus me'. An attitude of curiosity allows us to listen to another's point of view with openness and respect for differences. Neither of us is the problem; the dispute or unresolved issues becomes the problem. So we should unite in tackling the common enemy.

Shift from being defensive and aggressive to being empathic and assertive

A defensive or aggressive climate escalates conflict. In this mode there is normally a tendency to make the people the problem. When we use empathic and assertive approaches, it's more likely that we can establish a collaborative environment and focus on the issues that are really causing the conflict in the first place. When we depersonalize a problem, we focus on the issue rather than the people. Our focus turns from blaming others towards understanding them instead.

Shift from win-lose to win-win

Stop thinking about keeping a scoreboard. Shifts must occur in our ways of thinking, as well as our words and actions. Ultimately, our style will be determined by the combination of our attitudes and behaviours.

Our thoughts create our reality. Everything begins with a thought. If we become more aware of our thoughts and feelings, then we can start to understand the process and work with the mind to generate a more positive outcome. At this point we will truly understand ourselves, and be able to exercise choice about what goes on in our heads and how we act as a consequence. When we understand we are 80 percent responsible for the way people treat us we will be more inclined to give respect. Then *we* will be respected.

IT'S TIME... to embrace conflict. Remember, everything you resist will persist. If you don't overcome the conflict with the particular person or situation then that lesson will come around again until that lesson is learnt.

Communicating with compassion

We live in the age of communication. So many of us have a collection of cellphones, laptops and various other gadgets that connect us to a world of information in an instant. Channel hopping, 'Googling' and using Facebook have all become favourite pastimes and it's commonplace these days to video-conference with people from all around the world. The technology today is amazing, making the degree of communication available to us greater then ever before. We are all available and connected. But just think, are we really connected?

Are we truly communicating? Or have we, in fact, lost the subtle art of connecting with another human being from the level of the heart in favour of simply living in a world of noise and pictures? How much value do we really give to the spoken word when it truly comes from a place of the heart and the spirit?

In fact, how we communicate with others, and how we receive from others, depends a great deal upon our sense of self-worth. An online chat with dozens of friends may give us a sense of power and self-esteem for a moment, but it is far more courageous and fulfilling to listen – to really listen – to the human being that is in front of us and venture into a genuine conversation and relationship. When we embark on a method of communication that is more than superficial and distant, we may even be able to touch the soul of another and ignite the light of love, creativity, happiness and joy.

First and foremost it is important to ensure that the attitudes and feelings behind our words are always of goodwill. It takes self-understanding and self-esteem to be able to do this, but in order to maintain good relationships, and to resolve any conflict or misunderstanding, the inner work of respecting both ourselves and the other party is essential. If we don't like or respect who we are dealing with, they will pick this up, in our communication.

It is true that up to 90 percent of the messages we convey to others are expressed non-verbally through our, largely unconscious, body language. Our actual words only form a tiny percentage of our communication. Therefore, our true feelings will definitely reveal themselves, whether we choose to or not, when we are face to face with another person.

Words, and the intentions behind them, carry a subtle form of energy. Whatever we send out inevitably comes back to us like a boomerang. If we find ourselves thinking negatively about someone, watch out, because at some point it will be coming back to us.

A heart that is filled with pain, sorrow and discontentment will almost always be complaining, usually with bitterness or resentment bubbling just below the surface. True communication is then impossible, because one party will be busy proclaiming their misery or attempting to get their needs met, while the other party is either busy competing for their attention, or will have just switched off and shut down or gone home. Thus, many of our conversations these days are not so much a dialogue but more like two monologues happening at the same time.

Likewise, an argument can never be communication because it lacks the essential ingredients of compassion, equality and the ability to listen to and understand one another. We create contests out of our need to be right, but in fact we are both entrenched in a losing battle.

The aim of inner work is to heighten our awareness, and to learn who we are and how we function. It is to challenge our own beliefs, attitudes and approaches; *that* is the inner work we have to do. When we fail to do this, it is this that creates problems for us in developing healthy relationships with ourselves and others. The more we know about ourselves, the more we will be able to understand others.

An enlightened soul will be able to speak many languages in order to communicate with others: the language of the heart, the soul, and the eyes. All of these are deeply experienced in a place of inner silence.

IT'S TIME... to communicate from the heart with love. To speak through the lips with uplifting words, and to communicate through the eyes with an attitude that has only the best intention for others. Not even cyberspace can ignite this kind of pure attitude and energy. For this sort of experience in life we have to become real; that means we have to be present here. Let's put our heart and soul back into being present, then maybe we will start to see compassion in our communication.

Oiling the squeaky vision

Have you ever heard the expression, 'The squeaky wheel gets the oil'? Well, believe it or not, 'squeakers' and complainers do achieve results; mountains are moved as a result of mild but persistent squeakiness.

For those on the receiving end of a complaint the immediate reaction is often not very well received. Some use the evasive approach by switching off, saying, "Oh, it has nothing to do with me. It's not my fault." For others it creates hopelessness "What's the point in doing anything? I might as well give up." Then there are those who begin to join the 'squeakers and groaners' club "Yes, you are absolutely right, nothing works around here!"

It's no surprise that we are put off by complaints; on the surface they don't sound very constructive and can make us feel annoyed, angry, resentful or hopeless. We strive day and night to make our world 'picture perfect' but don't always succeed. When others complain about us, or the way we do things, we feel inadequate and insecure and we say to ourselves 'Well, I have done all that I can, what more can I do?' We take it personally, we shrivel up inside and wonder 'What's the point?'

But, there is another approach to handling complaints and criticism. When someone is complaining it's usually because they feel that their vision of the end result is better than ours, or they feel the need to correct us because they feel we have strayed from our aim. In the heat of the moment, when words are spoken passionately, we have to focus on the vision, otherwise the end result gets lost. We tend to project most of our energy in fixing the problem that caused the complaint, rather than trying to understand the real reason for the complaint or criticism and whether it was useful or not. We don't recognize that if we could only step back from our emotional response for a moment, we could gain an understanding of what the complainer is really reflecting back to us. If we could do this, then maybe we could even learn something.

If we listen to the complaints that come our way with dispassion we will notice that, in reality, both parties share the same vision. Both are looking for the best possible result, but are looking from different angles. Take a few moments to paraphrase what you hear them say, such as "So you would like to see a cleaner, quieter environment around here?" Ask yourself "Why would this person be saying this?" This way, opposition is diffused, and competition turns into collaboration. From this new standpoint you may even realize that the squeaks in the relationship are an opportunity in disguise giving us a signal to come back to a state of compassion, understanding and growth.

IT'S TIME... to be tolerant of other people's complaints, not defensive. Try to understand their point of view and what are they saying, just as we would like them to understand our point of view. With time, we can master these squeaks, oil the wheels of our relationships, and achieve the best result for all concerned. Suddenly the above expression takes on a whole new meaning as we take time to oil our vision rather than just trying to fix the wheel.

Love is the only weapon

Once upon a time there was a wise man who insisted that to live well, one had to be positive, forgiving and be thankful for all of life. One day, a traveller came to him and asked, "How can I be positive? Nothing is going right in my life. I have been badly hurt by people I trusted, and now I want revenge!"

The wise man shook his head and asked "What would you do to those who have hurt you?"

The traveller replied "I'd tear them from limb to limb … I'd ruin their business … I'd …," with all the pain and sorrow pouring from his heart, he then cried "Can you help me to get revenge?"

"Yes," said the wise man. "I'll certainly help you, but first you must do two things for me."

"I will. I will do anything." the traveller said.

"First," said the wise man, "I want you to tear a branch off that tree over there."

The traveller readily went to the tree and twisted off a large branch. "There you are! What's the second thing?"

The wise man smiled and said "Now, put it back."

The traveller stood staring at the wise man and said "I can't do that."

"No?" asked the wise man. "So then remember this. It's very easy to wound and to destroy, but it is more difficult to repair the damage that has been done."

Many a time we want to take revenge on people who have hurt us. But, although the tree will go on to grow another branch and bear more fruits, with human relationships it's a

little more difficult to withdraw words or rewind actions. In moments of retribution it is best to take a few quiet moments to oneself before committing to a course of punishment.

A moment of self-reflection will show that in times of hurt, the only thought that will bring peace of mind is to learn from the lesson and to move on. Continue to maintain the positive frame of mind that we are not doing it for the other party; we are doing it for ourselves.

When one has been around the cycles of hurt, pain, revenge, hurt, pain, revenge, one starts to realize there is no end to these cycles. It is an infinite creation of waste and negative thoughts, which will most likely destroy you, rather than the other party. Revenge only boils the blood of hatred and creates upheaval and restlessness in the mind, inhibiting any expression of goodness in the soul which could help the healing process.

IT'S TIME... to ask yourself which path are you following: reconciliation or revenge? The only weapon worth carrying is love. Although the ego may try and convince you to fight and win the battle, if you hold onto love you will in fact be winning the war.

W–righting away

Assessing your progress on the spiritual path is not easy and requires deep honesty, and the courage to look within. Putting your thoughts down on paper can give you a fresh perspective and help you to view your life's journey clearly, perhaps even save you from entering dark alleys and taking unnecessary detours.

The activity of writing is a process that helps de-clutter the mind and release issues that may have been buried for a long time. As people begin this type of creative process they find their thinking becomes clearer and sharper. Thoughts become more concentrated and they are able to make decisions with clarity and conviction.

Journaling, or putting your thoughts down on a daily basis is an excellent method of soothing the past and healing emotional wounds. Sometimes in a relationship, when nothing more can be said or done and you are still simmering in your pain over a betrayal and your broken heart, it's a good idea to make the journal your companion. When your friends are tired of hearing your broken record, then speak to your journal. It's the most faithful friend you will ever have.

In the process, frustrations are placed on paper – or on the laptop – rather than on our relationships. Anger is vented with the pen rather than a weapon. We feel better for freeing ourselves from the bitterness in private rather than in public.

Writing of this nature where there is little thinking required and you can just dump your thoughts in a safe place, can best be done in the morning as soon as you awaken. Throughout the night the active and busy mind has been conjuring thoughts and replaying scenarios through our dreams. The subconscious contains a mine of information, some of which will surface in the morning to reveal the important things that need to be dealt with in your life. When we get too caught up in our early morning routines we miss these valuable insights.

Ideas will appear, determination will get stronger, enthusiasm will be revived, viewpoints will be clearer, beliefs strengthened and creativity will emerge. You will feel a deeper sense of freedom and a connection with you, the soul.

Some experts say it's best to put your journal away for a few months and not read what you have written. But if you truly want to understand what comes to the surface through your writing, then there is no time like the present. Why wait for months to re-track your thoughts and feelings?

For you to feel totally comfortable writing away, or 'w-righting' away, it's best to keep your journal – your private pal – somewhere safe and away from prying eyes. It's best not to show it to others, as the fear of being judged may prevent you

from letting your true nature and honest thoughts and feelings emerge and slow you down on your road to recovery.

You can use your writing when you need to address confrontations. First, write down what you might say to the other person, or define issues that you might bring up. Reading it out loud may help you to see if you would like to take a different approach. For example, would it be better to be quiet and non-confrontational in this case? Use your journal as your mediator and you may just find you resolve conflicts more peacefully.

Be careful, however, that writing does not take the place of actual conversation. Sometimes there is a vital need to communicate and anyone can write a note to another, thereby avoiding the real issues or the person in question. Notes are not magicians who can make your problems disappear. The real work of facing your trials and tribulations in a considered, calm and courageous way will increase your capacity to deal with things better and bring peace to your heart and to your soul.

IT'S TIME... to get it all down on paper and to invoke your own inner psychologist, therapist and healer. Writing allows you to voice frustrations and to bring your deepest feelings and emotions to the surface, to reveal your inner demons and to help face them. It can create inspiration and give you a fresh outlook on your spiritual journey. The process of 'inking your thinking' might be all you need to put 'w-right your life'.

Bringing closure

Bringing closure in personal relationships is very important. It allows us to move on peacefully with a lightness of spirit, fewer negative thoughts and hopefully with no regrets or grudges. Yet expecting closure can also be a futile exercise at times. Sometimes, we have to accept that the only closure we may get is by closing the door behind us as we walk away.

Every story has an ending. No movie or play would be complete without those final words: 'The End'. So, don't fret if you are pursuing closure as it's natural and normal. Bringing completion creates clarity in our life. Once we know where we stand in regard to people and places, we know where to take off from again.

Not all endings, however, are happily ever after and we may have to agree to disagree. We may never see eye to eye with that person and that's also OK. At least we can be at peace knowing we tried, so try before giving up. Acceptance, and not rejection of the situation is important before we can move on. Don't push to fix things in the relationship if it's not happening naturally, as this just aggravates the situation. Remind yourself that suffering is a choice.

There are some people who use the silent treatment as a control mechanism in their relationships and deem that as closure. Silence used in this way does not always bring peace of mind. The philosophy of karma teaches us that karma has to be cleared on the same level in which it was created, because we have to come back to a place of balance. If it was created in the mind, then one can clear it with pure thoughts. If it is created through words, then an apology is imperative. If it is done through actions, then silence definitely cannot counteract the action. A positive deed has to replace the negative one. We need humility to bring closure on the level in which it was created.

Very often the inner work of moving on in the mind is the hardest step. Learning to let go in the mind is the first step toward closure. Sometimes we want a divorce but won't let go of all the baggage and blame. That would be akin to cutting only the branches when really we need to burn the roots. Once we decide we want to let go and move on, then 80 percent of the work has already been achieved. If we are expectant or waiting for something more from our 'drama' then we have not truly let go and are not seeking closure. Honesty with the self is necessary here for closure to take place.

Closure really means that one chapter has closed and we are ready to begin a new one. Karol K. Truman talks with clarity about the subject of feelings in her book, *Feelings Buried Alive Never Die*. It's almost as though one has to acknowledge each and every feeling within us to be able to move on. Each one of us has to take complete responsibility for the way we feel. If we are caught in the blame game then we will be waiting for the other party to fix us, or our situation, and we will be left powerless. In which case we will be forever putting commas, instead of full stops in our life and never reaching a point of closure.

Closure cannot take place in a state of weakness, it can only happen in a state of fullness. Maturity and realization are two of the stages that are implicit within the process of closure. Just as within nature a seed will naturally detach from its fruit once it ripens. If we are still feeling raw, then closure, in other words, the ripening or healing, needs more time. In that case, perhaps a closer look at the situation is required, maybe some more forgiveness is needed together with acceptance and humility.

Become a leader of your own life and take action. Don't always wait for things to happen to you because sometimes they never will. You may have to take the first step in opening a dialogue and asking the right questions to finish any unfinished business. Life passes by for people who wait for things to happen. It's like sitting on the fence and avoiding taking a decision for fear of failure. When we sit on the fence for too long, the indecisiveness can be both painful and unpleasant.

Take time to write or paint your thoughts. Write without judging the writing or even reading it again. Write a play, poem or short story and create the ending you would have liked to have seen. Paint a picture to express your feelings. These writings or paintings can be major eye openers to help us realize our mistakes and to prevent us from repeating them again.

Another exercise that can help to get things off your chest is letter writing – but a letter that you will never actually send to the person, because you are just writing for yourself. This allows you to express everything you ever wanted to without actually causing more damage to yourself, people and the relationship.

Sometimes creating rituals around 'The End' can help us bring things to a close more easily. For example, taking time to create a bonfire to burn that letter. Or burying all the stuff they have given to you as presents under your favourite tree or corner of the garden, or give those things away and let the pain go away with them. Make the process symbolic for you. Invite friends to come and sit in a sacred circle, light a candle and announce to them that you are making a new life with a fresh new start.

IT'S TIME... to take heed and bring closure to certain areas of your life. See what is working and what is not; don't waste more time and energy. Learn to let go and move on. Once you feel satisfied with the ending that you have created, then it really is the end of the problem.

Conclusion

Relationships are what animate our lives – they are the very stuff of life. Without them we would not exist, or life would cease to be worth living. However, although our relationships give our lives meaning and purpose, they can also cause us extreme joy or pain and every shade of emotion in between. Managing our relationships is not always an easy process.

Throughout these articles I have explored the deeper, spiritual aspects of relationships. I have looked at how we can create and maintain healthy relationships, how we can overcome some of the problems we may encounter along the way, and even how we can bring closure where necessary.

Imagine a world where each human being lived in accordance with their highest spiritual principles of love, respect, trust, honesty and integrity. It would be a very different world from what we see around us today. This may be a world we would all like to see, but even though we would all subscribe and aspire to these common principles, few of us have the power to put them into practise.

Learning to handle our relationships in the right way is a spiritual art we can develop, and the philosophy of Raja Yoga meditation makes learning these arts of life simple, possible and practical. The process begins by knowing that we already have all of the necessary resources within us to create peaceful, caring and harmonious relationships, and we also have the strength to overcome adversity. When we realize this we will not only be able to control our negative emotions, we will also be able to transform them.

For someone who is prepared to do the work necessary to develop these qualities and consciously create good relationships, it should be said that it takes time, determination and patience. It takes effort to override the old, negative conditioning and patterns of behaviour. It takes courage to face our inner demons, it takes self-respect to let go of our expectations of ourselves and others, and it takes humility to let go of our habit of taking sorrow from other people's hurtful comments and actions. However, the ultimate reward is guaranteed a hundred times greater than whatever effort we make.

The important thing is to remain aware and to always remember to reconnect with our inner positive core values. Then our responses will come from that deeper place; a calm, loving and peaceful place where we can choose to respond rather than react, being mindful of the consequences of our actions, and to act appropriately from a place of balance. If we pay attention to create harmony within ourselves, this will naturally be reflected in our relationships and in our lives. These changes also will have a positive impact on the environment and the world around us.

An even more important thing to realize is that it all starts with you and me. We have to take responsibility. We have to take the initiative. If we wait for others to change, we may wait forever.

If you choose to take up this challenge, then I wish you the very best for your journey. You are on the road to building a better life for yourself and a better world too.

About the author

Aruna is fortunate to have the blend of both cultures – the East and West! She was born in Nakuru (Kenya), educated in London (England), worked in Vancouver (Canada), and has lived in various other parts of the world and travels regularly to India.

Aruna was exposed to spiritual truths from an early age; in fact she had her first meditation experience at the tender age of 8. By the age of 14 she had found her calling and decided to focus on what mattered most in life– the development of her soul journey. For the past 36 years, Aruna has been studying the gentle art of Raja Yoga Meditation taught by Brahma Kumaris World Spiritual University (www.bkwsu.org). She is currently one of their experienced teachers, travelling regularly to promote the work of the university, running retreats, managing projects, teaching and facilitating in the areas of human development and writing weekly articles.

She has also helped establish meditation centres in Canada, Turkey, Bahrain and Kuwait. Aruna is a Certified Negotiator in Conflict Resolution and together with her degree in natural health continues to promote a peaceful, natural and vegetarian lifestyle.

To learn more about It's Time Blog go to www.arunaladva.org or email: info@arunaladva.org.

References

"*Codependency*" Mental Health America. Web. 12 September 2012. (*http://mentalhealthamerica.net/go/codependency*)

"*Codependency*" Wikipedia: The Free Encyclopedia. Wikimedia Foundation Inc. 25 August 2012. Web. 12 September 2012. (http://en.wikipedia.org/wiki/Codependency)

"*Conflict resolution*" The Centre for Conflict Resolution Training, Justice Institute of British Columbia, 1996

Saul, John Ralston, *The Unconscious Civilization*, 1999

Schussler, Steven, *It's a Jungle in There: Inspiring Lessons, Hard-Won Insights, and Other Acts of Entrepreneurial Daring*, 2010

Truman, Karol K., *Feelings, Buried Alive Never Die*, 2007

About Raja Yoga

Raja Yoga is an ancient system of bringing the mind and emotions into balance in order to develop knowledge and wisdom and to gain a deep understanding of the self. Through the simple practice of silent meditation and by turning your consciousness inward you can bring the mind and emotions into balance and become the creator of your own thoughts and feelings.

About the Brahma Kumaris

The Brahma Kumaris is a network of organisations in over 100 countries, with its spiritual headquarters in Mt Abu, India. The University works at all levels of society for positive change. Acknowledging the intrinsic worth and goodness of the inner self, the University teaches a practical method of meditation that helps people to cultivate their inner strengths and values.

The University also offers courses and seminars in such topics as positive thinking, overcoming anger, stress relief and self-esteem, encouraging spirituality in daily life. This spiritual approach is also brought into healthcare, social work, education, prisons and other community settings.

The University's Academy in Mount Abu, Rajasthan, India, offers individuals from all backgrounds a variety of life-long learning opportunities to help them recognise their inherent qualities and abilities in order to make the most of their lives.

All courses and activities are offered free of charge. Visit www.brahmakumaris.org for more information.

www.inspiredstillness.com

How and where to find out more

SPIRITUA L HEADQUAR TERS
PO Box No 2, Mount Abu 307501, Rajasthan, India
Tel: (+91) 2974-
238261 to 68
Fax: (+91) 2974-238883
E-mail: abu@bkivv.org

**INTERNATIONAL CO-ORDINATING OFFICE &
REGIONAL OFFICE
FOR EUROPE AND THE MIDDLE EAST**

Global Co-operation House, 65-69 Pound Lane,
London, NW10 2HH, UK
Tel: (+44) 20-8727-3350
Fax: (+44) 20-8727-3351
E-mail: london@brahmakumaris.org

REGIONAL OFFICES

AFRICA
Global Museum for a Better World, Maua Close,
off Parklands Road, Westlands
PO Box 123, Sarit Centre, Nairobi, Kenya
Tel: (+254) 20-374-3572
Fax: (+254) 20-374-3885
E-mail: nairobi@brahmakumaris.org

AUSTRALIA AND SOUTH EAST ASIA
A181 First Ave, Five Dock,Sydney,2046 Australia
E-mail: ashfield@au.brahmakumaris.org

THE AMERICAS AND THE CARIBBEAN
Global Harmony House, 46 S. Middle Neck Road,
Great Neck, NY 11021, USA
Tel: (+1) 516-773-0971
Fax: (+1) 516-773-0976
E-mail: newyork@brahmakumaris.org

RUSSIA , CIS AND THE BALTIC COUNTRIES
Brahma Kumaris World Spiritual University
2, Lobachika, Bldg. No. 2
Moscow – 107140
RUSSIA
Tel: (+7) : +7499 2646276
Fax: (+7) 495-261-3224
E www: brahmakumarisru.com
 www: spiritual-development.ru
E-mail: moscow@brahmakumaris.org

For publications visit:-

www.Inspiredstillness.com

E-mail: enquiries@bkpublications.com

It's Time...

Soul Journey & Personal Development